New Directions for
Child and Adolescent
Development

MW01252036

Elena L.
Grigorenko
EDITOR-IN-CHIEF

William Damon
FOUNDING EDITOR

Attachment in Middle Childhood: Theoretical Advances and New Directions in an Emerging Field

Guy Bosmans
Kathryn A. Kerns

EDITORS

Number 148 • Summer 2015
Jossey-Bass
San Francisco

ATTACHMENT IN MIDDLE CHILDHOOD: THEORETICAL ADVANCES AND NEW
DIRECTIONS IN AN EMERGING FIELD
Guy Bosmans, Kathryn A. Kerns (eds.)
New Directions for Child and Adolescent Development, no. 148
Elena L. Grigorenko, Editor-in-Chief

Microfilm copies of issues and articles are available in 16 mm and 35 mm,
as well as microfiche in 105 mm, through University Microfilms, Inc., 300
North Zeeb Road, Ann Arbor, Michigan 48106-1346.

ISSN 1520-3247   electronic ISSN 1534-8687

NEW DIRECTIONS FOR CHILD AND ADOLESCENT DEVELOPMENT is part of The
Jossey-Bass Education Series and is published quarterly by Wiley
Subscription Services, Inc., a Wiley company, at Jossey-Bass, One
Montgomery Street, Suite 1200, San Francisco, CA 94104-4594. Post-
master: Send address changes to New Directions for Child and Adoles-
cent Development, Jossey-Bass, One Montgomery Street, Suite 1200, San
Francisco, CA 94104-4594.

New Directions for Child and Adolescent Development is indexed in Cam-
bridge Scientific Abstracts (CSA/CIG), CHID: Combined Health Informa-
tion Database (NIH), Contents Pages in Education (T&F), Educational
Research Abstracts Online (T&F), Embase (Elsevier), ERIC Database
(Education Resources Information Center), Index Medicus/MEDLINE
(NLM), Linguistics & Language Behavior Abstracts (CSA/CIG), Psycho-
logical Abstracts/PsycINFO (APA), Social Services Abstracts (CSA/CIG),
SocINDEX (EBSCO), and Sociological Abstracts (CSA/CIG).

INDIVIDUAL SUBSCRIPTION RATE (in USD): $89 per year US/Can/Mex,
$113 rest of world; institutional subscription rate: $416 US, $456
Can/Mex, $490 rest of world. Single copy rate: $29. Electronic only–all
regions: $89 individual, $416 institutional; Print & Electronic–US: $98
individual, $500 institutional; Print & Electronic–Canada/Mexico:
$98 individual, $540 institutional; Print & Electronic–Rest of World:
$122 individual, $574 institutional.

COVER PHOTOGRAPHS: ©iStock.com/paulaphoto (top); ©iStock.com/vm
(middle); ©iStock.com/ericsphotography (bottom)

EDITORIAL CORRESPONDENCE should be e-mailed to the editor-in-chief:
Elena L. Grigorenko (elena.grigorenko@yale.edu).

Jossey-Bass Web address: www.josseybass.com

Contents

1

Attachment in Middle Childhood: Progress and Prospects

Guy Bosmans, Kathryn A. Kerns

Abstract

Contrary to the substantial amount of research on infant, preschool, adolescent, and adult attachment, middle childhood has long been neglected by the international attachment research community. In the past two decades, however, there has been a steep increase in research focusing on middle childhood attachment. This article provides an overview of past research, with a focus on the characteristics of secure versus insecure attachment at this age period, and an understanding of the different approaches to measure attachment. The article demonstrates the relevance of past middle childhood attachment research for both developmental psychologists and clinicians trying to understand the importance of middle childhood in individuals' development across the life span. © 2015 Wiley Periodicals, Inc.

NEW DIRECTIONS FOR CHILD AND ADOLESCENT DEVELOPMENT, no. 148, Summer 2015 © 2015 Wiley Periodicals, Inc.
Published online in Wiley Online Library (wileyonlinelibrary.com). • DOI: 10.1002/cad.20100

T he study of parent–child attachment has been a vibrant area of research. Initially the field focused on the idea that a key development in infancy is the child's opportunity to form a relationship with a caregiver who meets the child's physical and emotional needs (Ainsworth, Blehar, Waters, & Wall, 1978; Bowlby, 1969). An outcome of protective, sensitive care is that the child comes to use the parent as a secure base from which to explore and as a safe haven in times of stress. The child also develops a cognitive model of the caregiver as supportive and loving and a model of the self as worthy of love. In addition, a secure attachment relationship fosters the development of the child's social and emotional competence as it provides a context for learning about relationships (e.g., how to care for others and be cared for) and self-regulation (e.g., how to regulate emotions, resolve conflicts with peers; Brumariu, Article 3; Moss & Lecompte, Article 5, both this issue) and supports children's exploration of the world (e.g., the ability to benefit from learning at school; Verschueren, Article 6, this issue).

From empirical studies we now know a great deal about factors that promote the development of secure attachment in infancy (e.g., sensitive and responsive care) and its long-term developmental correlates (e.g., positive self-concept, better peer relationships, fewer behavioral problems, and anxiety). Yet Bowlby (1969) argued that attachment is important across the life span. There has been extensive exploration of attachment in adolescence (Allen, 2008). Contrary to developmental chronology, the last developmental period studied by attachment researchers has been middle childhood (Kerns & Brumariu, in press), yet there are important reasons to study attachment at this age. The developmental outline of attachment will be incomplete without studies that identify the key features and correlates of attachment in middle childhood. Studies of attachment in middle childhood have relevance for longitudinal studies of child adaptation, as biological and social developments occurring at this age (e.g., Del Giudice, Article 2, this issue) likely provide the foundation for problems emerging in adolescence (e.g., delinquency, depression). Hence, middle childhood studies on attachment development and its sequelae have proven to have significant theoretical and clinical relevance.

Over the past 15 years, there has been a growing number of studies on middle childhood attachment. This issue provides a timely opportunity to evaluate the state of the field, discussing both what we have learned and gaps in our understanding. In this introductory article, we focus on the features of attachment during the middle childhood years and review measurement approaches. Given the rapid expansion of research on this topic and space concerns, referencing is frequently illustrative rather than exhaustive (see other articles in this issue, and Kerns & Brumariu, in press, for more extensive presentations of individual research findings).

NEW DIRECTIONS FOR CHILD AND ADOLESCENT DEVELOPMENT • DOI: 10.1002/cad

Parent–Child Secure Attachment in Middle Childhood

Main, Kaplan, and Cassidy (1985) proposed that evidence for attachment processes should be identifiable on the levels of observable attachment behavior and of attachment representations. Evidence has been found for both levels in middle childhood research. At the first level, Kerns and Brumariu (in press) identified several defining features that are typical for the attachment behavioral system in middle childhood. First, the goal of the attachment system changes from *proximity* to the attachment figure in early childhood to the *availability* of the attachment figure in middle childhood. This reflects the fact that children are less often in need of parental assistance due to a growth in self-regulation skills. It is still necessary, however, for children to feel they can access the caregiver when needed.

Second, parents remain the primary attachment figures for children in middle childhood. When asked about situations likely to invoke the need for an attachment figure, even 11- to 12-year-old children show a strong preference for parents over peers (e.g., Seibert & Kerns, 2009). Although peers are important members of children's social networks, they generally do not serve as attachment figures (as they begin to do by late adolescence; Allen, 2008). Instead, prematurely relying on peers to fulfill attachment needs is generally associated with poorer developmental outcomes (Allen, 2008). Moreover, research also suggests that some of the conditions that elicit support-seeking behavior (e.g., pain and illness, separation, and anxiety) remain largely the same as in infancy. Interestingly, academic failure and social conflict become important, suggesting that adolescent themes are gradually emerging in this age group (Vandevivere, Braet, & Bosmans, 2015).

Third, there is a shift toward greater coregulation of secure base contact between the child and parent figure with the emergence of a supervisory partnership between the parent and child (Kerns, Aspelmeier, Gentzler, & Grabill, 2001; Waters, Kondo-Ikemura, Posada, & Richters, 1991). By the end of middle childhood, the attachment between parent and child can be viewed as a collaborative alliance whereby the child is still relying on the stronger, wiser parent figure but is also beginning to use the parent as a resource rather than relying on the parent to solve the child's problems (Kerns & Brumariu, in press).

Finally, attachment figures continue to function both as *safe havens* in time of distress as well as *secure bases* that support a child's exploration. They promote a child's confidence in tackling challenges and in experimentation in spite of risk to fail (Heylen et al., 2014). Fathers may be especially likely to function as secure bases that support children's exploration by providing encouragement for exploration (Bretherton, 2010).

At the level of representations, the internal working models of securely attached children in middle childhood consist of a similar secure base script as was found in adults (Psouni & Apetroaia, 2014; Waters, Bosmans,

Vandevivere, Dujardin, & Waters, in press). This cognitive script consists of a causal chain of expected events. The script starts with the expectation that the attachment figure will notice distress or that the child can seek support during distress. Then the attachment figure provides emotional and practical support to alleviate distress, and the child feels supported and returns to normal activities. This script is important because it assimilates information during interactions with parents in line with secure attachment expectations. Children who trust in parents as a secure base will continue to experience trust over time. By contrast, children who lack secure base trust will fluctuate in their trust appraisals over time—for example, after a conflict, their trust decreases (Bosmans, Van de Walle, Goossens, & Ceulemans, 2014).

Middle childhood research shows that this assimilation effect can be explained by trust-related information processing biases. Children who trust less in the availability of their mother interpret maternal behavior in a more negative way, even if the mother's behavior could be interpreted as supportive (De Winter, Salemink, & Bosmans, 2014). Also, less trusting children remember more negative interactions with mother at the expense of remembering positive interactions with her (Dujardin, Bosmans, Braet, & Goossens, 2014). Finally, the attention of insecurely attached children is automatically overly focused on mother, at the expense of exploration and support seeking (Bosmans, Braet, Koster, & De Raedt, 2009; Bosmans, Braet, Heylen, & De Raedt, 2015).

Taken together, middle childhood research at the representational level provides a coherent understanding of the secure base script-related mechanisms that guide children's day-to-day interactions with attachment figures. These findings are promising for at least two reasons. First, they are in line with findings in adolescent and adult attachment research (Dykas & Cassidy, 2011), suggesting developmental consistency from middle childhood to adulthood. Second, they add to adult attachment information processing research by demonstrating the functions of these processes (e.g., they influence support-seeking behavior and stability in attachment expectations). Thus, middle childhood research gradually helps in unraveling one of the most fundamental black boxes in Bowlby's attachment theory (Zimmermann & Iwanski, Article 4, this issue).

This line of research is only emerging, and many challenging questions remain. Most important, research on cognitive schema development suggests that schemas are still under development in childhood and early adolescence, influenced by new experiences. It is only later in adolescence that these schemas become crystallized into a cognitive diathesis that robustly alters individuals' responses to context cues (Allen, 2008). Future research should try to unravel the course of attachment schema development as this might help explain the limited longitudinal stability of attachment (Pinquart, Feußner, & Ahnert, 2013) and the impressive treatment effects obtained after restoring trust in the parent–child dyad (Diamond et al., 2010). Finally, an intriguing question could be whether information processing biases affect the ability of insecurely attached adolescents and adults to provide a coherent (i.e., internally consistent, realistic, and appropriately elaborated) discourse of their attachment experiences.

These studies also raise the question of which factors contribute to the development and maintenance of secure attachment in middle childhood. The literature with younger children has documented that a caregiver's provision of responsive, sensitive care and a warm emotional climate is related to secure attachment (Ainsworth et al., 1978). In middle childhood, studies show that responsive, warm care remains related to secure attachment (e.g., Kerns, Brumariu, & Seibert, 2011; Moss, St.-Laurent, Dubois-Comtois, & Cyr, 2005; Scott, Riskman, Woolgar, Humayun, & O'Connor, 2011). In contrast to infancy, in middle childhood, children are beginning to assert more autonomy. Thus, sensitive care at this age also seems to involve allowing them to express their own feelings and opinions (Kerns et al., 2011).

In addition to environmental influences, biological factors might start influencing attachment development in middle childhood (see also Del Giudice, Article 2, this issue). Compared to infancy, parent–child relationships might be more shaped by the complex dynamics of gene–environment interactions, suggesting larger effects of genetic variation on attachment (in)security at older ages. For example, onset of middle childhood can be considered a biological switch that increases children's awareness of (gender-related) social dynamics, leading to the accelerated development of secure base scripts (e.g., Del Giudice, Article 2, this issue).

Insecure Attachment Patterns in Middle Childhood

Although we have a rather clear developmental outline of secure attachment in middle childhood and what changes from early childhood onward, we know less about the distinctive features of insecure attachment patterns at this age. Avoidant attachment emerges when parents have been rejecting of children's bids for care and contact. Avoidantly attached children may become overly self-reliant and fail to seek care as a way to maintain a relationship with a rejecting caregiver. Ambivalent attachment (also called preoccupied attachment) develops when children have experienced inconsistent care and thus become chronically uncertain about the availability of caregivers. Their uncertainty leads them to focus on their attachment figures and to frequently engage in attachment behaviors as a strategy to maintain their caregiver's attention and involvement. Disorganized attachment is thought to develop when children lack access to a reliable and responsive attachment figure due to the experience of harsh parental care or a psychologically unavailable caregiver (e.g., parent is overwhelmed and distracted). As a consequence, the child lacks a stronger, wiser attachment figure and responds either by failing to develop any consistent strategy toward the caregiver or by taking control of the relationship (role reversal).

NEW DIRECTIONS FOR CHILD AND ADOLESCENT DEVELOPMENT • DOI: 10.1002/cad

Research on specific insecure attachment patterns in middle childhood (see Brumariu, Article 3; Moss & Lecompte, Article 5, both this issue) has been guided primarily by work on the manifestation of insecure patterns in younger children, with relatively little attention to age changes in insecure attachment patterns. There has been discussion of changes in disorganized attachment, in that the controlling type is thought to emerge in middle childhood (Moss et al., 2005), but there has been little consideration of developmental transformations for the avoidant or ambivalent patterns. An exception is the speculations by Hans, Bernstein, and Sims (2000) regarding the ambivalent pattern. Although they acknowledge that ambivalent children will continue to show exaggerated displays of negative emotion as a way to elicit care, they argue that a new manifestation in middle childhood is that ambivalent children might begin to provoke caregivers and initiate conflict as another way to engage with an inconsistently available caregiver. For avoidant children, diminished communication may be a distinguishing feature, with the exception that parents and children might continue to communicate about child accomplishments (e.g., school achievements). Thompson and Raikes (2003) suggested that the field should be open to the possibility that new forms of insecure attachment may emerge at older ages. A direction for future research would be studies that focus on identifying age-related changes in the insecure attachment patterns. A challenge in doing so, however, is the lack of clear conceptualization of how different insecure patterns might change across development. Thus, there is a need in future work to develop and test expanded theorizing about insecure patterns and how they may change in middle childhood (see also Del Giudice, Article 2, this issue) as well as how they are related to children's adaptation (see Articles 2–6).

Middle Childhood Attachment Research: Methodological Challenges for Attachment Research and Theory

Attachment research at other ages often developed a preference for specific measurement approaches. Infant attachment is preferentially measured through observation of parent–child interactions (e.g., the Strange Situation Procedure [SSP]; Ainsworth et al., 1978). In the preschool years, both behavioral observation and narrative techniques such as story stems (Bretherton, Ridgeway, & Cassidy, 1990) have been used. In adolescence and adulthood, attachment is measured through autobiographical interviews (e.g., the Adolescent/Adult Attachment Interview; Main et al., 1985) or questionnaires (e.g., the Experiences of Close Relationships questionnaire; Brenning, Soenens, Braet, & Bosmans, 2012). In middle childhood, a large number of methods and specific measures have been developed to assess attachment, and there is no dominant measurement approach.

The broad variety of attachment measures likely reflects the fact that middle childhood was the last period studied, and many of the available measures were adapted from measures that were used in both earlier and later developmental periods (Kerns & Seibert, in press). Our expanding research experience shows that middle childhood is a developmental period that challenges the assumptions underlying the measures that were developed for other developmental periods. Compared to younger ages, short separations from mother no longer elicit distress or the immediate need for proximity and reassurance (Main & Cassidy, 1988), which makes it difficult to develop behavioral measures of attachment that rely on separation–reunion procedures, although behavioral observation techniques have been developed to assess attachment in 6- to 8-year-olds (e.g., Bureau & Moss, 2010; Easterbrooks, Bureau, & Lyons-Ruth, 2012). Compared to older ages, there are more concerns that children could be somewhat limited in their capacity to reflect on their relationships, as is required by attachment autobiographical interviews.

Driven by these developmental concerns, initial middle childhood attachment research (particularly on children over 8 years of age) mainly focused on two types of representational measures of attachment: questionnaires (e.g., Kerns et al., 1996, 2001) and narrative storytelling assessments (e.g., Bureau & Moss, 2010; Granot & Mayseless, 2001; Kerns, Tomich, Aspelmeier, & Contreras, 2000). Most used and best validated is the Security Scale (SS; Kerns et al., 1996). Other questionnaires followed (e.g., a child version of the Inventory of Parent and Peer Attachment, Ridenour, Greenberg, & Cook, 2006; a child version of the Experiences of Close Relationships Revised, Brenning et al., 2012), but all had high correlations with the original SS ($rs > .60$, Bosmans, Braet, Soenens, & Verschueren, 2008; Brenning et al., 2012). However, while designing the SS, the authors were wary of possible validity concerns related to hypothesized difficulties to consciously access internal working models through self-report and related to risk for response bias and social desirability (Kerns et al., 1996). This led the authors to suggest that alternative measures should also be used to study middle childhood attachment.

In response to this suggestion, a first movement toward developing alternative measures was the adaptation of Bretherton et al.'s (1990) story stem procedure (e.g., Granot & Mayseless, 2001). Story stems provide children with initial story prompts that introduce a problem (e.g., child is hurt or upset). Children are provided physical props (dolls and other items), and asked to show and tell what happens next in the story. The story coding takes into account how the parent figure is portrayed, how emotions are regulated, how problems are addressed, and the coherence in children's narratives. Story stem procedures have been used successfully in several studies. For example, children who tell secure stories show better adaptation at school and with peers (Granot & Mayseless, 2001), are more successful at regulating their emotions (Brumariu, Article 3, this issue), and experience more accepting and less psychologically controlling parenting and fewer internalizing problems (Kerns et al., 2011).

NEW DIRECTIONS FOR CHILD AND ADOLESCENT DEVELOPMENT • DOI: 10.1002/cad

In recent years, more translational and creative work has been done to design alternative tests to measure middle childhood attachment. Many of these measures are still based on analyzing attachment narratives. Middle childhood versions of the Adult Attachment Interview have been developed based on the assumption that children may be able to report about recent experiences with caregivers, with less securely attached children reporting less accepting experiences with attachment figures and failing to narrate coherently on their attachment relationships (the Friends and Family Interview [FFI], Kriss, Steele, & Steele, 2012; the Child Attachment Interview [CAI], Borelli et al., 2010; Shmueli-Goetz, Target, Fonagy, & Datta, 2008). Although these techniques are promising, there is a need for further validation, especially in relation to parenting and to other measures of attachment. Most recently, middle childhood versions of the Secure Base Script Assessment test have been developed to identify which children recognize secure base script information in a verbal prompt outline (Psouni & Apetroaia, 2014; Waters et al., in press). In this procedure, children are presented with a word list and asked to tell a story using the words. A securely attached child will recognize the implied secure base script and tell a story in which a problem emerges that is solved through the intervention of the mother with a positive resolution to the situation. There are also efforts under way to develop observational coding systems for 9- to 12-year-olds that can be used to code attachment patterns. Unlike observational approaches for 6- to 8-year-old children that are based on separation–reunion procedures (Bureau & Moss, 2010; Easterbrooks et al., 2012), approaches with older children are based on observations of mother–child interaction when dyads are engaging in challenging conversations (Brumariu, Kerns, Bureau, & Lyons-Ruth, 2013). In another approach to observed behavior, Bosmans et al. (2015) found that insecurely attached children waited longer to call for mother's support when failing to solve a puzzle they had been told that peers managed to solve. Finally, Bosmans and colleagues (e.g., Bosmans et al., 2009) pioneered the use of performance-based measures of attachment that assess attachment through cognitive information processing (e.g., patterns of attention to the mother under stress). For most of these newer middle childhood attachment measures, much validation work is left to do (Kerns & Seibert, in press).

Although all these measures have contributed to the contemporary knowledge base of middle childhood attachment, the discussion is ongoing regarding which can be considered the gold standard measure for middle childhood attachment. In addition, there are questions regarding how highly attachment measures that use different approaches "should" be correlated and which available measures would be best to use to validate new approaches. A difficulty is that most studies in middle childhood (as found in the larger attachment literature) only use a single measure of attachment (for exceptions, see Bureau & Moss, 2010; Kerns et al., 2000, 2011; Psouni & Apetroaia, 2014). This discussion is also fueled by longitudinal studies showing, for example, that infant maternal sensitivity is more strongly linked with adolescent narrative attachment measures than to adolescent self-report attachment measures (Steele et al., 2014).

Building on our experience of using a variety of measurement strategies, we propose a perspective shift in the discussion. We argue that the main question should not be "Which is the golden standard measure?" but rather "Which component or aspect of the attachment construct is measured?" Our argumentation is in line with current insights in other research areas. For example, in depression research, the consensus is increasingly reached that different measures of depression tap into different layers of the construct and do not necessarily need to correlate highly but rather need to be combined to get a more comprehensive understanding (Hankin, 2012). Applying such reasoning to attachment research requires asking what different attachment measures have in common and in what way might they be unique or specific.

Regarding the common core of attachment measures, Waters and Cummings (2000) argue that the secure base construct is the key to capturing attachment. Consequently, we would argue that all attachment measures should reflect whether individuals have the capacity to organize their interpersonal experiences and behavior to use a figure as a safe haven and secure base. Regarding the differences between separate attachment measures, dual process theory (e.g., Gawronski & Creighton, 2013) seems a promising theoretical framework that might reveal characteristics of each measure that are relevant to attachment theory.

According to dual process theory, measures differ to the extent that they tap into strategic or automatic processes. Measures of strategic processes, such as self-report measures, allow individuals to influence outcomes. Thus they give insight into the aspect of the attachment construct children are aware of and that reflects the way children want to present their attachment representations both to themselves and others. In middle childhood, measuring strategic processes could be especially valuable as children at this age tend to be concrete thinkers. Thus they may be more likely than adolescents to report actual experiences. In addition, in comparison to preschoolers, children in middle childhood may be better able to compare their experiences with those of others and thus have a more realistic view of their relationships (Stipek & Mac Iver, 1989). Measures of automatic processes focus on outcomes beyond an individual's strategic control (e.g., a child cannot decide whether to recount autobiographical memories in a coherent way or to focus attention more strongly to mother). Important to note here is that automatic versus strategic control reflects a dimensional difference and that all measures differ to the extent that they are more automatic or more strategic (Moors & De Houwer, 2006).

This conceptualization leads us to propose a simplified model for comparing measures of attachment in middle childhood (see Figure 1.1). Important in this figure is the fact that all measurement strategies have unique

Figure 1.1. Model of Measurement Approaches to Attachment in Middle Childhood

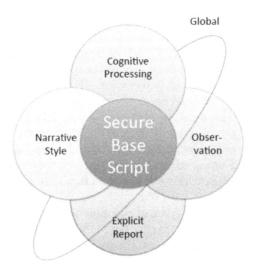

variance, but they all share a connection with the underlying secure base script. Although the model does not capture all aspects of attachment measurement, it does capture the fact that different approaches vary not only in the target of assessment (narrative style, cognitive information processing, observation, explicit report), but also vary on whether attachment is characterized as a quality of a particular relationship (e.g., father–child) or as a more general characteristic of the child.

Our conceptualization of the variation in attachment measures has significant implications for our understanding of attachment research in middle childhood and likely other ages. Most important, implied in dual process theory is the assumption that measures of strategic and automatic processes do not necessarily have to correlate or even should not correlate (Moors & De Houwer, 2006). This implication argues against the idea that there is only one gold standard approach to measure attachment and that lack of correlations between attachment measures is an indication that at least one of these measures is not attachment related. Instead, each measure might provide insight into specific components and mechanisms of the attachment system. Finally, this implication suggests that combining measures of both automatic and strategic attachment processes will provide a more comprehensive understanding of attachment-related outcomes.

Consequently, we believe that combining different measurement strategies should be the way forward for future attachment research. Currently, researchers from one research tradition tend to argue against findings revealed within other research traditions, believing in the supremacy of one measurement strategy. This occurs despite the fact that different measurement strategies show striking similarities in the processes uncovered (e.g., similar heightening and deactivation of emotions strategies have been found in observation and self-report research, Brenning et al., 2012; Brumariu, Article 3, this issue). Instead, our proposal is to use a comprehensive approach on attachment research measures in research.

Concluding Remarks

Middle childhood attachment research has provided an exciting new view on the mechanisms underlying longitudinal attachment development and the impact of attachment on children's resilience and vulnerabilities. We now know that in middle childhood, interactions with parents increasingly develop into secure base scripts and expectations that allow children to explore their social world with the certainty that their parents will not only provide care when needed but will also support exploration. Further, insecurely attached children's emerging maladaptive emotion regulation strategies and cognitive biases put them at risk of developing social difficulties or psychopathology. These findings also call for the development of treatment strategies focusing specifically on restoring middle childhood attachment relationships. The research presented in this issue should be considered a valuable knowledge base, enabling the design of such treatment strategies. Finally, this introduction also showed the challenges of operationalizing attachment in middle childhood. Future attachment research might benefit from developing a coherent and conceptually sound framework to understand the specific meaning of different attachment measures. This article has taken a first step toward developing such a framework by applying dual process theory to attachment measures. Although some preliminary studies show that combining measures of strategic and automatic processes provide a more subtle and improved understanding of attachment-related outcomes (Bosmans, Koster, Vandevivere, Braet, & De Raedt, 2013), more research is now needed to investigate this framework.

With these insights, middle childhood attachment research can inform clinical practice. For example, classical cognitive-behavioral therapy treatment programs focus on the acquisition of emotion regulation skills. Adding programs that focus on improving parenting skills have shown limited utility, and an approach focused on restoring attachment ruptures may be more fruitful. Moreover, this research suggests that it is possible to enhance children's developmental outcomes by creating a context with supportive and responsive partners like teachers and peers who may be able to provide support in the absence of parental attachment figures (Seibert & Kerns, 2009; Verschueren, Article 6, this issue).

References

Ainsworth, M. D. S., Blehar, M. C., Waters, E., & Wall, S. (1978). *Patterns of attachment: A psychological study of the strange situation.* Oxford, UK: Erlbaum.

Allen, J. P. (2008). The attachment system in adolescence. In J. Cassidy & P. R. Shaver (Eds.), *Handbook of attachment: Theory, research, and clinical applications* (2nd ed., pp. 419–435). New York, NY: Guilford Press.

Borelli, J. L., Crowley, M. J., David, D. H., Sbarra, D. A., Anderson, G. M., & Mayes, L. C. (2010). Attachment and emotion in school-aged children. *Emotion, 10*(4), 475–485.

Bosmans, G., Braet, C., Heylen, J., & De Raedt, R. (2015). Children's attentional processing of mother and proximity seeking. *PLOS ONE.* doi:10.1371/journal.pone.0124038

Bosmans, G., Braet, C., Koster, E., & De Raedt, R. (2009). Attachment security is linked with attentional breadth in middle childhood. *Journal of Clinical Child and Adolescent Psychology, 38,* 872–882.

Bosmans, G., Braet, C., Soenens, B., & Verschueren, K. (2008). [Psychometric evaluation of attachment questionnaires in a Flemish sample]. Unpublished raw data.

Bosmans, G., Koster, E. H. W., Vandevivere, E., Braet, C., & De Raedt, R. (2013). Young adolescent's confidence in maternal support: Attentional bias moderates the link between attachment-related expectations and behavioral problems. *Cognitive Therapy and Research, 37,* 829–839.

Bosmans, G., Van de Walle, M., Goossens, L., & Ceulemans, E. (2014). (In)variability of attachment in middle childhood: Secure base script evidence in diary data. *Behaviour Change, 31,* 225–242.

Bowlby, J. (1969). *Attachment and loss: Vol. 1. Attachment.* New York, NY: Basic Books.

Brenning, K., Soenens, B., Braet, C., & Bosmans, G. (2012). Attachment and depressive symptoms in middle childhood and pre-adolescence: Testing the applicability of the emotion regulation model of attachment. *Personal Relationships, 19*(3), 445–464.

Bretherton, I. (2010). Fathers in attachment theory and research: A review. *Early Child Development and Care, 180*(1–2), 9–23.

Bretherton, I., Ridgeway, D., & Cassidy, J. (1990). Assessing internal working models of the attachment relationship. In M. T. Greenberg, D. Cicchetti, & E. M. Cummings (Eds.), *Attachment in the preschool years: Theory, research, and intervention* (pp. 273–308). Chicago, IL: University of Chicago Press.

Brumariu, L. E., Kerns, K. A., Bureau. J.-F., & Lyons-Ruth, K. (2013). *Middle childhood attachment strategies coding system (Version 1).* Unpublished manual.

Bureau, J.-F., & Moss, E. (2010). Behavioural precursors of attachment representations in middle childhood and links with social adaptation. *British Journal of Developmental Psychology, 28,* 657–677.

De Winter, S., Salemink, E., & Bosmans, G. (2014). *Training attachment-related interpretation bias: Examining the causal effect of interpretation bias on attachment expectations.* Manuscript under review.

Diamond, G. S., Wintersteen, M. B., Brown, G. K., Diamond, G. M., Gallop, R., Shelef, K., & Levy, S. (2010). Attachment-based family therapy for adolescents with suicidal ideation: A randomized controlled trial. *Journal of the American Academy of Child and Adolescent Psychiatry, 49*(2), 122–131.

Dujardin, A., Bosmans, G., Braet, C., & Goossens, L. (2014). Attachment-related expectations and mother-referent memory bias in middle childhood. *Scandinavian Journal of Psychology, 55*(4), 296–302.

Dykas, M. J., & Cassidy, J. (2011). Attachment and the processing of social information across the life span: Theory and evidence. *Psychological Bulletin, 137*(1), 19–46.

Easterbrooks, M. A., Bureau, J., & Lyons-Ruth, K. (2012). Developmental correlates and predictors of emotional availability in mother–child interaction: A longitudinal study from infancy to middle childhood. *Development and Psychopathology, 24,* 65–78.

Gawronski, B., & Creighton, L. A. (2013). Dual process theories. In D. E. Carlston (Ed.), *The Oxford handbook of social cognition* (pp. 282–312). New York, NY: Oxford University Press.

Granot, D., & Mayseless, O. (2001). Attachment security and adjustment to school in middle childhood. *International Journal of Behavioral Development, 25*, 530–541.

Hankin, B. L. (2012). Future directions in vulnerability to depression among youth: Integrating risk factors and processes across multiple levels of analysis. *Journal of Clinical Child and Adolescent Psychology, 41*(5), 695–718.

Hans, S., Bernstein, V. J., & Sims, B. E. (2000). Change and continuity in ambivalent attachment relationships from infancy through adolescence. In P. M. Crittenden & A. H. Claussen (Eds.), *The organization of attachment relationships: Maturation, culture, and context* (pp. 277–299). New York, NY: Cambridge University Press.

Heylen, J., Bosmans, G., Vasey, M., Dujardin, A., Vandevivere, E., Braet, C., & De Raedt, R. (2014). *Attachment and effortful control: Relationships with maladjustment in middle childhood.* Manuscript under review.

Kerns, K. A., Aspelmeier, J. E., Gentzler, A. L., & Grabill, C. M. (2001). Parent–child attachment and monitoring in middle childhood. *Journal of Family Psychology, 15*, 69–81.

Kerns, K. A., & Brumariu, L. E. (in press). Attachment in middle childhood. In J. Cassidy & P. Shaver (Eds.), *Handbook of attachment* (3rd ed.). New York, NY: Guilford Press.

Kerns, K. A., Brumariu, L. E., & Seibert, A. C. (2011). Multi-method assessment of mother–child attachment: Links to parenting and child depressive symptoms in middle childhood. *Attachment and Human Development, 13*, 315–333.

Kerns, K. A., Klepac, L., & Cole, A. (1996). Peer relationships and preadolescents' perceptions of security in the child-mother relationship. *Developmental Psychology, 32*, 457–466.

Kerns, K. A., & Seibert, A. C. (in press). Finding your way through the thicket: Promising approaches to assessing attachment in middle childhood. In E. Waters, B. Vaugn, & H. Waters (Eds.), *Measuring attachment.* New York, NY: Guilford Press.

Kerns, K. A., Tomich, P. L., Aspelmeier, J. E., & Contreras, J. M. (2000). Attachment-based assessments of parent–child relationships in middle childhood. *Developmental Psychology, 36*, 614–626.

Kriss, A., Steele, H., & Steele, M. (2012). Measuring attachment and reflective functioning in early adolescence: An introduction to the Friends and Family Interview. *Ricerca in Psicoterapia/Research in Psychotherapy: Psychopathology, Process and Outcome, 15*(2), 87–95.

Main, M., & Cassidy, J. (1988). Categories of response to reunion with the parent at age 6: Predictable from infant attachment classifications and stable over a 1-month period. *Developmental Psychology, 24*, 415–426.

Main, M., Kaplan, N., & Cassidy, J. (1985). Security of infancy, childhood, and adulthood: A move to the level of representation. In I. Bretherton & E. Waters (Eds.), Growing points of attachment theory and research. *Monographs of the Society for Research in Child Development, 50*(1–2, Serial No. 209), 66–104.

Moors, A., & De Houwer, J. (2006). Problems with dividing the realm of cognitive processes. *Psychological Inquiry, 17*, 199–204.

Moss, E., St.-Laurent, D., Dubois-Comtois, K., & Cyr, C. (2005). Quality of attachment at school age: Relations between child attachment behavior, psychosocial functioning, and school performance. In K. A. Kerns & R. A. Richardson (Eds.), *Attachment in middle childhood* (pp. 189–211). New York, NY: Guilford Press.

Pinquart, M., Feußner, C., & Ahnert, L. (2013). Meta-analytic evidence for stability in attachments from infancy to early adulthood. *Attachment & Human Development, 15*(2), 189–218.

Psouni, E., & Apetroaia, A. (2014). Measuring scripted attachment-related knowledge in middle childhood: The Secure Base Script Test. *Attachment & Human Development*, 16, 22–41.

Ridenour, T. A., Greenberg, M. T., & Cook, E. T. (2006). Structure and validity of people in my life: A self-report measure of attachment in late childhood. *Journal of Youth and Adolescence*, 35, 1037–1053.

Scott, S., Riskman, J., Woolgar, M., Humayun, S., & O'Connor, T. G. (2011). Attachment in adolescence: Overlap with parenting and unique prediction of behavioral adjustment. *Journal of Child Psychiatry and Psychology*, 52, 1052–1062.

Seibert, A. C., & Kerns, K. A. (2009). Attachment figures in middle childhood. *International Journal of Behavioral Development*, 33, 347–355.

Shmueli-Goetz, Y., Target, M., Fonagy, P., & Datta, A. (2008). The Child Attachment Interview: A psychometric study of reliability and discriminant validity. *Developmental Psychology*, 44(4), 939–956.

Steele, R. D., Waters, T. E. A., Bost, K. K., Vaughn, B., Truitt, W., Waters, H. S., . . . Roisman, G. I. (2014). Caregiving antecedents of secure base script knowledge: A comparative analysis of young adult attachment representations. *Developmental Psychology*, 50(11), 2526–2538.

Stipek, D., & Mac Iver, D. (1989). Developmental change in children's assessment of intellectual competence. *Child Development*, 60, 521–538.

Thompson, R. A., & Raikes, H. (2003). Toward the next quarter-century: Conceptual and methodological challenges for attachment theory. *Development and Psychopathology*, 15(3), 691–718.

Vandevivere, E., Braet, C., & Bosmans, G. (2015). Under which conditions do early adolescents need maternal support? *Journal of Early Adolescence*, 35(2), 162–169.

Waters, E., & Cummings, E. (2000). A secure base from which to explore close relationships. *Child Development*, 71(1), 164–172.

Waters, E., Kondo-Ikemura, K., Posada, G., & Richters, J. E. (1991). Learning to love: Mechanisms and milestones. In M. Gunnar & L. A. Sroufe (Eds.), *Minnesota Symposium on Child Psychology: Vol. 23. Self processes in early development* (pp. 217–255). Hillsdale, NJ: Erlbaum.

Waters, T. E. A., Bosmans, G., Vandevivere, E., Dujardin, A., & Waters, H. S. (in press). Secure base representations in middle childhood across two cultures: Associations with parental attachment representations and maternal reports of behavior problems. *Developmental Psychology*.

GUY BOSMANS *is an assistant professor in the Parenting and Special Education Research Group at the University of Leuven, Belgium.*

KATHRYN A. KERNS *is a professor in the Department of Psychological Sciences at Kent State University, Kent, OH.*

Del Giudice, M. (2015). Attachment in middle childhood: An evolutionary–developmental perspective. In G. Bosmans & K. A. Kerns (Eds.), *Attachment in middle childhood: Theoretical advances and new directions in an emerging field. New Directions for Child and Adolescent Development, 148*, 15–30.

2

Attachment in Middle Childhood: An Evolutionary–Developmental Perspective

Marco Del Giudice

Abstract

Middle childhood is a key transitional stage in the development of attachment processes and representations. Here I discuss the middle childhood transition from an evolutionary–developmental perspective and show how this approach offers fresh insight into the function and organization of attachment in this life stage. I begin by presenting an integrated biological model of middle childhood and discussing the neurobiological mechanisms that support the middle childhood transition. I examine the potential role of adrenal androgens, focusing on their activational effects in interaction with early exposure to sex hormones. I then discuss three insights arising from the integrated model and apply them to the development of attachment in middle childhood. I consider the changing functions of attachment in light of social competition, the emergence of sex differences in attachment, and the model's implications for the genetics of attachment in middle childhood. © 2015 Wiley Periodicals, Inc.

I
n the long arc of attachment from the cradle to the grave, middle childhood stands out as a phase of change and transformation. It is the time
when attachment relationships undergo a decisive shift toward mutual
co-regulation, multiple working models start to get integrated into general
representations, and affectional bonds with caregivers and family members
lose their exclusive nature as children begin to form close relationships with
same-aged peers (Kerns, 2008; Mayseless, 2005).

Despite the importance of these developmental transitions, understanding the nature and functioning of attachment in middle childhood
has proven a difficult, elusive task. While the methodological challenges
of research in this age group have undoubtedly played a part (Kerns, 2008;
Kerns, Schlegelmilch, Morgan, & Abraham, 2005), I believe there is also a
deeper theoretical reason. Since its inception, attachment theory has been
rooted in a sophisticated model of the evolved functions of infancy, cen-
tered on the dynamic balance between the need for protection and that
for learning and exploration. Likewise, extensions of attachment theory
to adolescence and adulthood have benefited from a well-developed understanding of the biological and motivational processes associated with
sexual maturation and the beginning of mating, pair bonding, and reproduction. However, a comparable functional model of middle childhood has
been lacking until very recently, leaving a gap in the theory's foundations
and preventing the emergence of a true life span perspective on attachment
development.

Fortunately, things are changing fast. In the past two decades, our understanding of middle childhood has been revolutionized by converging
theories and findings from anthropology, evolutionary psychology, prima-
tology, endocrinology, and behavior genetics. I recently showed how this
body of work can be synthesized to yield an integrated, evolutionary–
developmental model of middle childhood (Del Giudice, 2014). My goal
in this article is to reconsider the role of attachment in middle childhood
from an evolutionary–developmental perspective, using insights from the
integrated model to make sense of existing findings and suggest directions for advancement. In particular, I argue that social competition in middle childhood contributes to explain developmental change in attachment
styles; that sexual selection (i.e., selection arising from mate choice and
competition for mates) explains the evolution of sex differences in attachment and their emergence in middle childhood; and that an evolutionary–
developmental perspective helps make sense of the genetics of attachment
across the life course.

An Integrated Model of Middle Childhood

In this section, I present an overview of middle childhood from a biological
perspective. In particular, I discuss the hormonal changes that take place
in the transition from early to middle childhood and their function in the

development of individual and sex differences. I conclude the section with three insights into the nature of middle childhood.

The Nature of Middle Childhood. Middle childhood is one of the main stages of human development, roughly corresponding to what is called juvenility in other primates. While juveniles are still sexually immature, they are no longer strictly dependent on parents for survival. The beginning of middle childhood in humans is marked by the onset of androgen secretion by the adrenal glands (adrenarche) in both sexes around 6 to 8 years of age (Bogin, 1997). By age 6, the brain has almost reached its maximum size, and receives a decreasing share of the body's glucose after the consumption peak of early childhood (Kuzawa et al., 2014). The energy diverted away from brain development is employed to increase muscle mass and deposited as fat in preparation for sexual maturity (the adiposity rebound; Hochberg, 2008; see Figure 2.1). Whereas brain growth slows down in middle childhood, brain development is still well under way, with fast-paced synaptogenesis in cortical areas (gray matter) and rapid maturation

Figure 2.1. Developmental Trajectories of Human Growth and Sex Hormones Production, From Conception to Adolescence.

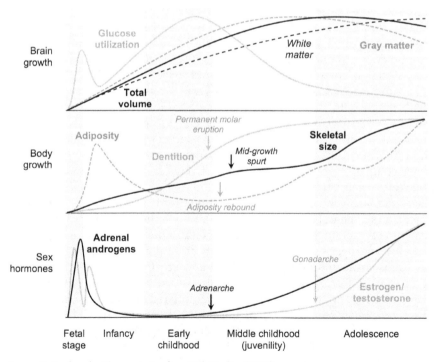

Source: Reproduced with permission from Del Giudice (2014).
Arrows show the landmark events that characterize middle childhood.

New Directions for Child and Adolescent Development • DOI: 10.1002/cad

of axonal connections (white matter; see Giedd & Rapoport, 2010; Figure 2.1). In primates and other mammals, juvenility is a phase of intensive social learning—often accomplished through play—in which youngsters practice adult patterns of behavior and acquire essential social and foraging skills (Joffe, 1997; Walker, Burger, Wagner, & Von Rueden, 2006). In humans, middle childhood is marked by a global reorganization of cognitive functioning known as the 5-to-7 shift (Weisner, 1996), with a simultaneous and striking increase in perceptual abilities, motor control, memory, complex reasoning skills, self-regulation, mentalizing, and moral reasoning (reviewed in Del Giudice, 2014).

Cross-culturally, middle childhood is the time when children are expected to start providing active help in domestic tasks—taking care of younger siblings, collecting food and water, tending animals, and so forth (Bogin, 1997; Lancy & Grove, 2011; Weisner, 1996). In favorable ecologies where food can be gathered with little risk and no need for sophisticated skills, juveniles can make a substantial contribution to family subsistence (Kramer, 2011). Cross-culturally, the transition to middle childhood is typically associated with a strong separation in gender roles; even in societies where tasks are not rigidly assigned by sex, middle childhood is marked by a peak in spontaneous sex segregation and sexually differentiated play (see Del Giudice, Angeleri, & Manera, 2009). At a broader social level, cross-cultural evidence shows that juveniles start "getting noticed" by adults—that is, they begin to be viewed as persons with their own individuality and social responsibility (Lancy & Grove, 2011). In total, two major interlocking functions of middle childhood are *social learning* and *social integration* in a system of roles, norms, activities, and shared knowledge.

Adrenarche and Adrenal Androgens. Around 6 to 8 years of age—with much individual variation and only minor differences between the sexes—adrenal glands begin to secrete increasing amounts of androgens, mainly dehydroepiandrosterone (DHEA) and dehydroepiandrosterone sulfate (DHEAS; Auchus & Rainey, 2004; Hochberg, 2008). Adrenal androgens have comparatively minor influences on physical development but powerful effects on brain functioning. DHEAS promotes neurogenesis and modulates glutamate and GABA (gamma-aminobutyric acid) receptors, the main mediators of neural excitation and inhibition in the brain; moreover, DHEA can directly act on androgen and estrogen receptors. Even more important, adrenal androgens can be converted to more potent sex hormones, such as testosterone and estrogen, in the brain (see Campbell, 2006; Del Giudice et al., 2009). As sex hormones, adrenal androgens play a twofold role (Figure 2.1): They *activate* sexually differentiated brain pathways that have been previously organized by the hormonal surges of prenatal development and infancy (e.g., brain networks that regulate aggression and sexual attraction), and they further *organize* brain development along sexually differentiated trajectories (Del Giudice et al., 2009). Moreover, adrenal androgens promote extended brain plasticity through synaptogenesis and may play an important role in shifting the allocation of the body's energetic resources away from brain development and toward the accumulation of muscle and fat (Campbell, 2006, 2011).

Adrenal androgens likely provide a major impulse for the psychological changes seen in middle childhood, including the emergence and intensification of sex differences in aggression, social play (including play fighting versus play parenting), and risk for psychopathology (Campbell, 2011; Del Giudice et al., 2009). Thanks to adrenarche—a feature shared with chimpanzees and, to some extent, gorillas (Bernstein, Sterner, & Wildman, 2012)—human development shows a peculiar pattern in which sexually differentiated brain pathways are activated several years before the development of secondary sexual characters. The resulting (temporary) decoupling between physical and behavioral development reinforces the idea of middle childhood as a sexually differentiated phase of social learning and experimentation (Geary, 2010).

The Transition to Middle Childhood as a Developmental Switch Point. In a broader evolutionary perspective, adrenarche can be reframed as a *developmental switch* (Del Giudice et al., 2009). A developmental switch (West-Eberhard, 2003) is a regulatory mechanism that activates at a specific point in development, collects input from the external environment and/or the state of the organism, and modulates the individual's developmental trajectory—ultimately resulting in the development of different *phenotypes* (morphological, physiological, and/or behavioral traits of an organism). For example, a switch may regulate the development of aggressive behavior so that safe conditions entrain the development of low levels of aggression, whereas threatening environments trigger high levels of aggression. Developmental switches enable *adaptive plasticity*—the ability of an organism to match its phenotype to the local environment in a way that promotes biological fitness (West-Eberhard, 2003). Plastic organisms track the state of the environment—usually through indirect cues—and use this information to develop alternative phenotypes that tend to promote survival and reproduction under different conditions.

An important aspect of developmental switches is that they integrate variation in the environment with individual differences in the genes that regulate the switches. For example, different individuals may have genetically different thresholds for switching between aggressive and nonaggressive phenotypes. This is known in the developmental literature as differential susceptibility to the environment (Belsky & Pluess, 2009). As well, the embodied effects of past experiences and conditions—for example, previous exposure to stress or nutritional scarcity—may modulate the functioning of a switch, allowing the organism to integrate information over time. In many cases, the effects of past experience on developmental switches may be mediated by epigenetic mechanisms (i.e., biochemical mechanisms that cause long-term changes in the expression of a gene without modifying its DNA sequence; see Meaney, 2010).

The concept of a developmental switch point resembles that of a *sensitive period*, in that the organism is maximally responsive to a specific environmental input. But there is a crucial difference: Since genetic and environmental inputs converge in the regulatory mechanism, a developmental switch amplifies both environmental *and* genetic effects on the phenotype (West-Eberhard, 2003). Indeed, the activation of a developmental switch exposes many potential sources of genetic variation, including genes involved in the regulatory mechanism and in the expression of the new phenotypes (see Del Giudice, 2014; Del Giudice et al., 2009).

My colleagues and I (Del Giudice et al., 2009; Del Giudice & Belsky, 2011) argued that the transition to middle childhood is a switch point in the development of *life history strategies*. Life history strategies are coordinate suites of morphological, physiological, and behavioral traits that determine how organisms allocate their resources to key biological activities such as growth, reproduction, mating, and parenting. At the level of behavior, individual differences in life history strategy are reflected in patterns of self-regulation, aggression, cooperation and prosociality, sexuality, and others (see Del Giudice et al., 2009; Del Giudice, Ellis, & Shirtcliff, 2011; Del Giudice, Gangestad, & Kaplan, in press; Ellis, Figueredo, Brumbach, & Schlomer, 2009).

While life history strategies are partly heritable, they also show a degree of plasticity in response to the quality of the environment, including the level of danger and unpredictability—embodied in the experience of early stress—and the availability of adequate nutritional resources. In a nutshell, environments that are dangerous and unpredictable (e.g., because of disease risk, violence, or social instability) tend to favor "fast" strategies characterized by early maturation and reproduction, sexual promiscuity, relationship instability, impulsivity, risk taking, aggression, and exploitative tendencies. In contrast, safe and predictable environment tend to entrain "slow" strategies characterized by late maturation and reproduction, stable relationships, high self-control, risk aversion, and prosociality. (Note that individual differences in life history reflect a continuum of faster to slower strategies rather than a rigid dichotomy between "fast" and "slow" types). Slow strategies are also favored by nutritional scarcity in absence of high levels of danger. (For a more detailed treatment, see Del Giudice et al., in press; Ellis et al., 2009.)

In this framework, adrenarche coordinates the expression of life history strategies by integrating individual genetic variation with information about the child's social and physical environment collected throughout infancy and early childhood. Adrenal androgens likely interact with the stress response system in this process. The stress response system—which includes the hypothalamic-pituitary-adrenal (HPA) axis as well as the sympathetic and parasympathetic autonomic branches—plays a major role in gathering and storing information about environmental safety, predictability, and resource availability. Adrenarche contributes to translate that information into adaptive, sexually differentiated patterns of behavior (Del Giudice et al., 2011). Consistent with this view, both early relational stress and early nutrition modulate the timing of adrenarche (Ellis & Essex, 2007; Hochberg, 2008). It is no coincidence that the first sexual and romantic attractions typically develop in middle childhood, at the same time when the frequency of sexual play increases dramatically (Bancroft, 2003; Herdt & McClintock, 2000).

By interacting with peers and adults, juveniles receive considerable feedback about the effectiveness of their nascent behavioral strategies. The information collected during middle childhood feeds into the next developmental switch point, that of gonadarche (the awakening of the testes/ovaries; see Ellis, 2013); the transition to adolescence offers a major opportunity to adjust or revise one's initial strategy before attaining full reproductive maturity (Del Giudice & Belsky, 2011).

Three Insights. The evolutionary–developmental model of middle childhood described in this section is outlined in Figure 2.2. Three important insights flow from the model's logic (Del Giudice, 2014). The first is that *social integration and social competition are complementary functions of middle childhood*. While evolutionary accounts of juvenility typically focus on learning, helping, and other forms of social integration, a life history approach emphasizes the need to consider social competition as well. In the peer group, children compete for vital social resources—status, reputation, allies, and friends. In fact, the social position achieved in middle childhood is a springboard for adolescence and adulthood; popularity and centrality within the peer network put a child at a considerable advantage, with potentially large effects on his or her ultimate reproductive success and, hence, biological fitness (Del Giudice et al., 2009).

Physical and relational aggression are obvious tactics for gaining influence, but social competition in the more general sense also occurs through prosocial behaviors, such as forming alliances, doing favors, displaying valuable skills, and others (Hawley, 2014). The centrality of social competition in middle childhood is reflected in the developmental trajectory of self-esteem: Whereas young children tend to report high levels of self-esteem with little individual variation, at around 7 to 8 years, many children experience a drop in self-esteem. As a result, middle childhood witnesses the emergence of substantial individual differences in self-evaluation that often persist through adolescence (Harter, 2006).

The second insight is that *sexual selection contributes to the emergence and intensification of sex differences in middle childhood*. By determining children's initial place in social networks and hierarchies, competition in middle childhood indirectly affects their future ability to attract sexual and romantic partners. For this reason, middle childhood is a likely target for sexual selection: Behavioral traits that increase competitive ability in middle childhood can be expected to spread in human populations because they indirectly increase an individual's success in mating and reproduction. Sexual

Figure 2.2. An Integrated Evolutionary–Developmental Model of Middle Childhood.

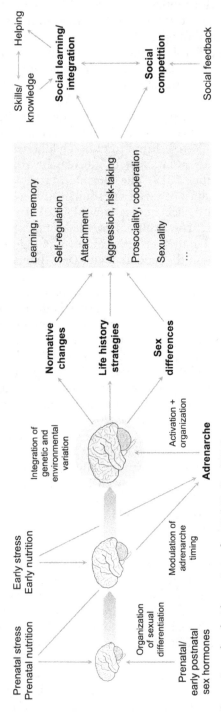

Source: Reproduced with permission from Del Giudice (2014).

selection is an important (if often overlooked) explanation for the emergence and intensification of sex differences in middle childhood. A prime example are sex differences in physical aggression, which increase at the beginning of middle childhood in tandem with sex differences in muscularity (which begin to appear in middle childhood), sex differences in play fighting (which peak in middle childhood), and sex differences in the onset of externalizing disorders (Del Giudice et al., 2009).

Finally, the role of adrenarche as a developmental switch implies that *in middle childhood, heightened sensitivity to the environment goes hand in hand with the expression of new genetic factors.* When adrenal androgens begin to rise during the transition to middle childhood, they activate a multiplicity of hormone-sensitive brain pathways that have remained dormant since infancy. In doing so, they release a certain amount of previously "hidden" genetic variation (Del Giudice et al., 2009). Thus, middle childhood should be characterized by a mixture of heightened sensitivity to the environment and expression of new genetic factors. Consistent with this prediction, twin studies have shown that the transition to middle childhood coincides with the onset of new genetic influences on prosocial and aggressive behaviors, intelligence, and verbal skills (reviewed in Del Giudice, 2014).

Implications for Attachment Theory

I now consider how the evolutionary–developmental model presented in the previous section can be applied to the development of attachment in middle childhood.

Social Competition and the Changing Functions of Attachment. Current views of attachment in middle childhood emphasize its role in fostering social integration. For example, Mayseless (2005) argued that a key evolutionary function of middle childhood is to start using peers as alternative attachment figures, thus initiating the shift from exclusive attachment to caregivers in infancy and early childhood to investment in peer relationships in adolescence and adulthood. However, peers are not just affiliation and cooperation partners but also competitors for social status and rewards. This dual role of peers can be expected to shape the functions of attachment in middle childhood and beyond.

The first implication of this expanded view is that attachment styles influence children's competitive strategies, both directly and indirectly. For example, anxious (preoccupied, ambivalent) styles may sensitize children to the possibility that their social partners will betray or exclude them and prompt a range of potentially effective countermeasures, including exaggerated displays of distress, requests for emotional and physical closeness, and relational aggression against potential "cheaters." In contrast, avoidant attachment may reduce a child's reliance on undependable partners and project an image of strength and independence that can be an asset in many social contexts. As relationships with peers take center stage, attachment styles should become less tailored to the characteristics of the child's care-givers and more attuned to the costs and benefits of different behaviors in the broader social environment. And since boys and girls differ system-atically in their strategies of affiliation and competition (Benenson, 2014; Geary, 2010), it is reasonable to predict that attachment styles will become sexually differentiated starting from middle childhood (more on this in the next subsection).

A related implication is that attachment in middle childhood should not be viewed only as a *predictor* of social variables such as aggression, prosociality, or externalizing and internalizing behaviors. Rather, attach-ment can be understood as one element in a suite of life history–related traits whose coordinated expression serves the biological goals of the child in his or her particular environment (Figure 2.2; see Simpson & Belsky, 2008). Early attachment relationships play a key role in shaping an indi-vidual's developmental trajectory; in a life history perspective, this is partly because they convey vital information about the safety and predictability of the environment (as well as the individual's value in the eyes of signif-icant others). In other words, attachment provides critical "input" to the systems that mediate life history development; as children grow up, how-ever, attachment styles become influenced by the "output" of the same sys-tems. While attachment security is moderately stable across development (e.g., Pinquart, Feußner, & Ahnert, 2013), specific attachment styles such as avoidance and ambivalence are much more subject to change (see Del Giudice, 2009). The longitudinal instability of attachment styles may be explained—at least in part—by the changing biological functions of attach-ment over the life course.

The correlates of insecure attachment in middle childhood include externalizing and other so-called pseudomature behaviors (Allen, Schad, Oudekerk, & Chango, 2014), such as precocious sexual and romantic en-gagement (Kerns, 2008; Sroufe, Bennett, Englund, Urban, & Shulman, 1993), as well as coercive tactics of social influence (Chen & Chang, 2012). A life history perspective suggests that these behaviors may reflect adaptive strategies tailored to harsh and/or unpredictable environments—strategies that necessarily entail a mixture of benefits and costs. The fact that imme-diate benefits, such as peer popularity and earlier access to sexual partners, tend to be short-lived compared with the lasting social and health costs of the same behaviors (Allen et al., 2014) is fully in line with the present-oriented focus of fast life history strategies. It is important to keep in mind that biological adaptation is ultimately driven by reproductive success; nat-ural selection does not necessarily promote psychological well-being or physical health and may even sacrifice survival in exchange for enhanced reproduction. Moreover, even adaptive developmental processes may result in genuinely maladaptive outcomes for some individuals (Frankenhuis & Del Giudice, 2012). It follows that the existence of psychological, social, or health costs does not automatically qualify a trait or behavior as maladaptive (see Ellis et al., 2012).

Sexual Selection and the Emergence of Sex Differences in Attachment. The general principle that sexual selection contributes to the emergence of sex differences in middle childhood can be extended to attachment styles. As I have argued in previous work (Del Giudice, 2009), the constellations of behaviors associated with different types of insecure attachment are likely to have different costs and benefits for boys and girls. In a nutshell, status and dominance are key reproductive resources for males; avoidant styles should help boys secure status through overt competition—though the risky nature of competition implies that there will be losers as well as winners (Frankenhuis & Del Giudice, 2012). In adulthood, attachment avoidance *minimizes commitment* in close relationships and supports investment in short-term sexual relationships. Human females face a different set of constraints, so that successful reproduction primarily requires securing sufficient material and social resources (e.g., a supportive network of relatives and friends). Anxious attachment emphasizes neediness and vulnerability and is characterized by constant preoccupation about the availability and commitment of one's partner. For these reasons, anxiety contributes to *maximize investment* of time and resources by relatives and partners—especially if the latter tend to be unreliable or uncommitted. Biological reasoning further suggests that sex differences should be small in safe and protected environments, increase at higher levels of stress, then decrease again in severely dangerous or unpredictable contexts (see Del Giudice, 2009, for details).

Studies of attachment in middle childhood that employ questionnaire measures systematically detect higher avoidance in boys and higher preoccupation in girls across cultures (Chen & Chang, 2012; Del Giudice, 2009). The same pattern is often observed in doll-play tasks, whereas interviews usually fail to reveal any significant sex differences (Bakermans-Kranenburg & van Ijzendoorn, 2009; Del Giudice, 2009; Kerns, Brumariu, & Seibert, 2011; Toth, Lakatos, & Gervai, 2013; Venta, Shmueli-Goetz, & Sharp, 2014). Taken together, these findings mirror those from studies of adult attachment. Meta-analytic evidence from romantic attachment questionnaires shows that men score higher than women in avoidance, whereas women are higher in anxiety (Del Giudice, 2011). When attachment state of mind is coded in discrete categories from the Adult Attachment Interview (AAI), no sex differences can be detected (Bakermans-Kranenburg & van Ijzendoorn, 2010). However, a recent study found that dimensional scores derived from the AAI reliably show significantly higher dismissiveness in men and higher preoccupation in women (Haydon, Roisman, Owen, Booth-LaForce, & Cox, 2014).

I recently showed that sex differences in romantic attachment become larger and more robust when the broad dimensions of avoidance and anxiety are split into narrower components or facets (Del Giudice, 2015).

Specifically, men score higher than women in *self-reliance*, whereas women score higher in *preoccupation* and *neediness*. These facets can be interpreted in an evolutionary perspective as strategies for minimizing commitment (self-reliance) and maximizing investment (preoccupation and neediness). The remaining two facets (labeled *discomfort with closeness* and *rejected desire for closeness*) do not have a straightforward interpretation in a life history framework and show a pattern of attenuated or reversed sex differences.

This move to the level of facets has promising implications for the study of attachment styles in middle childhood. As in adults, the size of sex differences may vary between facets of anxiety and avoidance, and assessment tools may differ in the balance of facets they tap. Also, a focus on facets might contribute to explain the modest concordance between attachment ratings obtained by different methods (e.g., questionnaires versus doll play; Kerns et al., 2011) and help identify the dimensions of variation that show the highest consistency across methods.

At the neurobiological level, adrenarche is likely to play a crucial role in the emergence of sex differences in attachment. In particular, I hypothesized that the activational effects of adrenal androgens would interact with the organizational effects of prenatal sex hormones to determine both individual and sex differences in attachment styles (Del Giudice, 2009). A recent study provided initial empirical support for this hypothesis (Del Giudice & Angeleri, 2015). In a sample of 285 Italian children aged 8 to 11 years, avoidant and preoccupied attachment styles were assessed with the Coping Styles Questionnaires (CSQ; Finnegan, Hodges, & Perry, 1996). Early exposure to sex hormones was indirectly assessed with an anatomical marker, the ratio of the length of the second and fourth finger of the right hand (2D:4D digit ratio). The digit ratio is a biomarker of the balance between testosterone and estrogen during fetal development (Manning, Kiduff, Cook, Crewther, & Fink, 2014; Ventura, Gomes, Pita, Neto, & Taylor, 2013). As expected, girls scored lower in avoidance and higher in preoccupation than boys; moreover, digit ratio was significantly associated with attachment scores within each sex, so that "feminized" digit ratios predicted lower avoidance and higher preoccupation in both boys and girls.

These findings provide the first demonstration of a link between prenatal exposure to sex hormones and sexually differentiated attachment styles in middle childhood. Future studies should integrate indicators of early exposure with direct measures of adrenal androgens in childhood. Another promising research topic is the association between adrenarche timing and individual trajectories in attachment styles from early to middle childhood.

Genetics of Attachment in Middle Childhood. Viewing the transition of middle childhood as a developmental switch point has intriguing implications for the genetics of attachment. In contrast with most psychological traits, individual differences in attachment styles in infancy and early childhood are heavily determined by children's environment and show little evidence of genetic effects (Bokhorst et al., 2003; O'Connor & Croft, 2001; Roisman & Fraley, 2008). While these findings leave some room for genotype-by-environment interactions (whereby children with different genotypes respond differently to the same environmental factors), the direct effect of genetic similarity in early life seems to be weak to negligible. The picture, however, changes dramatically in adolescence and adulthood: Both questionnaire and interview measures of adult attachment show a substantial role of genetic factors, with about 40% of individual variation explained by genetic similarity (Brussoni, Jang, Livesley, & Macbeth, 2000; Fearon, Shmueli-Goetz, Viding, Fonagy, & Plomin, 2014; Picardi, Fagnani, Nisticò, & Stazi, 2011; Torgersen, Grova, & Sommerstad, 2007).

In light of the theory and evidence presented here, the transition to middle childhood is likely to be the phase of development in which new genetic factors begin to significantly influence attachment styles. Also, the idea that sex hormones are implicated in the origin of both sex and individual differences in attachment styles in middle childhood suggests that future genetic research should target genes involved in sex hormones pathways (e.g., the genes that code for androgen and estrogen receptors) in addition to the standard candidate genes associated with oxytocin, dopamine, and serotonin pathways.

Conclusion

In this article, I showed how an evolutionary–developmental perspective can enrich current theoretical models of attachment in middle childhood and inform empirical research by suggesting novel, intriguing hypotheses. However, this discussion of the implications for attachment barely scratches the surface: The evolutionary–developmental approach is making headway in many other relevant areas, including developmental psychopathology (Del Giudice & Ellis, in press), and has much more to offer to mainstream attachment theory. Research on attachment in middle childhood has already made many important contributions, theoretical and empirical. However, I believe that it has not yet realized its full potential and that it will do so only by embracing a biological perspective and rediscovering its deep evolutionary roots.

References

Allen, J. P., Schad, M. M., Oudekerk, B., & Chango, J. (2014). What ever happened to the "cool" kids? Long-term sequelae of early adolescent pseudomature behavior. *Child Development, 85*, 1866–1880.

Auchus, R. J., & Rainey, W. E. (2004). Adrenarche—physiology, biochemistry and human disease. *Clinical Endocrinology, 60*, 288–296.

Bakersman-Kranenburg, M. J., & van Ijzendoorn, M. H. (2009). No reliable gender differences in attachment across the lifespan. *Behavioral and Brain Sciences, 33*, 22–23.

Bakermans-Kranenburg, M. J., & van Ijzendoorn, M. H. (2010). Invariance of adult attachment across gender, age, culture, and socioeconomic status? *Journal of Social and Personal Relationships, 27*, 200–208.

Bancroft, J. (Ed.). (2003). *Sexual development in childhood.* Bloomington: Indiana University Press.

Belsky, J., & Pluess, M. (2009). Beyond diathesis stress: Differential susceptibility to environmental influences. *Psychological Bulletin, 135*, 885–908.

Benenson, J. F. (2014). *Warriors and worriers: The survival of the sexes.* New York, NY: Oxford University Press.

Bernstein, R. M., Sterner, K. N., & Wildman, D. E. (2012). Adrenal androgen production in catarrhine primates and the evolution of adrenarche. *American Journal of Physical Anthropology, 147*, 389–400.

Bogin, B. (1997). Evolutionary hypotheses for human childhood. *Yearbook of Physical Anthropology, 40*, 63–89.

Bokhorst, C. L., Bakermans-Kranenburg, M. J., Fearon, R. M. P., van Ijzendoorn, M. H., Fonagy, P., & Schuengel, C. (2003). The importance of shared environment in mother-infant attachment security: A behavioral genetic study. *Child Development, 74*, 1769–1782.

Brussoni, M. J., Jang, K., Livesley, W. J., & Macbeth, T. M. (2000). Genetic and environmental influences on adult attachment styles. *Personal Relationships, 7*, 283–289.

Campbell, B. C. (2006). Adrenarche and the evolution of human life history. *American Journal of Human Biology, 18*, 569–589.

Campbell, B. C. (2011). Adrenarche and middle childhood. *Human Nature, 22*, 327–349.

Chen, B.-B., & Chang, L. (2012). Adaptive insecure attachment and resource control strategies during middle childhood. *International Journal of Behavioral Development, 36*, 389–397.

Del Giudice, M. (2009). Sex, attachment, and the development of reproductive strategies. *Behavioral and Brain Sciences, 32*, 1–21.

Del Giudice, M. (2011). Sex differences in romantic attachment: A meta-analysis. *Personality and Social Psychology Bulletin, 37*, 193–214.

Del Giudice, M. (2014). Middle childhood: An evolutionary-developmental synthesis. *Child Development Perspectives, 8*, 193–200.

Del Giudice, M. (2015). *Sex differences in romantic attachment: Zoom in to see the bigger picture.* Manuscript under review.

Del Giudice, M., & Angeleri, R. (2015). *Digit ratio (2D:4D) and attachment styles in middle childhood: Indirect evidence for an organizational effect of sex hormones.* Manuscript under review.

Del Giudice, M., Angeleri, R., & Manera, V. (2009). The juvenile transition: A developmental switch point in human life history. *Developmental Review, 29*, 1–31.

Del Giudice, M., & Belsky, J. (2011). The development of life history strategies: Toward a multi-stage theory. In D. M. Buss & P. H. Hawley (Eds.), *The evolution of personality and individual differences* (pp. 154–176). New York, NY: Oxford University Press.

Del Giudice, M., & Ellis, B. J. (in press). Evolutionary foundations of developmental psychopathology. In D. Cicchetti (Ed.), *Developmental psychopathology, Vol. 1: Theory and method* (3rd ed.). Hoboken, NJ: Wiley.

Del Giudice, M., Ellis, B. J., & Shirtcliff, E. A. (2011). The Adaptive Calibration Model of stress responsivity. *Neuroscience & Biobehavioral Reviews, 35*, 1562–1592.

Del Giudice, M., Gangestad, S. W., & Kaplan, H. S. (in press). Life history theory and evolutionary psychology. In D. M. Buss (Ed.), *The handbook of evolutionary psychology* (2nd ed.). Hoboken, NJ: Wiley.

Ellis, B. J. (2013). The hypothalamic-pituitary-gonadal axis: A switch-controlled, condition-sensitive system in the regulation of life history strategies. *Hormones and Behavior, 64*, 215–225.

Ellis, B. J., Del Giudice, M., Dishion, T. J., Figueredo, A. J., Gray, P., Griskevicius, V., ... Wilson, D. S. (2012). The evolutionary basis of risky adolescent behavior: Implications for science, policy, and practice. *Developmental Psychology, 48*, 598–623.

Ellis, B. J., & Essex, M. J. (2007). Family environments, adrenarche and sexual maturation: A longitudinal test of a life history model. *Child Development, 78*, 1799–1817.

Ellis, B. J., Figueredo, A. J., Brumbach, B. H., & Schlomer, G. L. (2009). The impact of harsh versus unpredictable environments on the evolution and development of life history strategies. *Human Nature, 20*, 204–268.

Fearon, P., Shmueli-Goetz, Y., Viding, E., Fonagy, P., & Plomin, R. (2014). Genetic and environmental influences on adolescent attachment. *Journal of Child Psychology and Psychiatry, 55*, 1033–1041.

Finnegan, R. A., Hodges, E. V. E., & Perry, D. G. (1996). Preoccupied and avoidant coping during middle childhood. *Child Development, 67*, 1318–1328.

Frankenhuis, W. E., & Del Giudice, M. (2012). When do adaptive developmental mechanisms yield maladaptive outcomes? *Developmental Psychology, 48*, 628–642.

Geary, D. C. (2010). *Male, female: The evolution of human sex differences*. Washington, DC: American Psychological Association.

Giedd, J. N., & Rapoport, J. L. (2010). Structural MRI of pediatric brain development: What have we learned and where are we going? *Neuron, 67*, 728–734.

Harter, S. (2006). Developmental and individual difference perspectives on self-esteem. In D. K. Mroczek & T. D. Little (Eds.), *Handbook of personality development* (pp. 311–334). Mahwah, NJ: Erlbaum.

Hawley, P. H. (2014). Ontogeny and social dominance: A developmental view of human power patterns. *Evolutionary Psychology, 12*, 318–342.

Haydon, K. C., Roisman, G. I., Owen, M. T., Booth-LaForce, C., & Cox, M. J. (2014). Shared and distinctive antecedents of adult attachment interview state-of-mind and inferred-experience dimensions. *Monographs of the Society for Research in Child Development, 79*(3), 108–125.

Herdt, G., & McClintock, M. (2000). The magical age of 10. *Archives of Sexual Behavior, 29*, 587–606.

Hochberg, Z. (2008). Juvenility in the context of life history theory. *Archives of Disease in Childhood, 93*, 534–539.

Joffe, T. H. (1997). Social pressures have selected for an extended juvenile period in primates. *Journal of Human Evolution, 32*, 593–605.

Kerns, K. A. (2008). Attachment in middle childhood. In J. Cassidy & P. R. Shaver (Eds.), *Handbook of attachment* (2nd ed., pp. 366–382). New York, NY: Guilford Press.

Kerns, K. A., Brumariu, L. E., & Seibert, A. (2011). Multi-method assessment of mother-child attachment: Links to parenting and child depressive symptoms in middle childhood. *Attachment & Human Development, 13*, 315–333.

Kerns, K. A., Schlegelmilch, A., Morgan, T. A., & Abraham, M. M. (2005). Assessing attachment in middle childhood. In K. A. Kerns & R. A. Richardson (Eds.), *Attachment in middle childhood* (pp. 46–70). New York, NY: Guilford Press.

Kramer, K. L. (2011). The evolution of human parental care and recruitment of juvenile help. *Trends in Ecology and Evolution, 26*, 533–540.

Kuzawa, C. W., Chugani, H. T., Grossman, L. I., Lipovich, L., Muzik, O., Hof, P. R., ... Lange, N. (2014). Metabolic costs and evolutionary implications of human brain development. *Proceedings of the National Academy of Sciences, 111*, 13010–13015.

Lancy, D. F., & Grove, M. A. (2011). Getting noticed: Middle childhood in cross-cultural perspective. *Human Nature, 22*, 281–302.

Manning, J., Kiduff, L., Cook, C., Crewther, B., & Fink, B. (2014). Digit ratio (2D:4D): A biomarker for prenatal sex steroids and adult sex steroids in challenge situations. *Frontiers in Endocrinology, 5*, 9.

Mayseless, O. (2005). Ontogeny of attachment in middle childhood: Conceptualization of normative changes. In K. A. Kerns & R. A. Richardson (Eds.), *Attachment in middle childhood* (pp. 1–23). New York, NY: Guilford Press.

Meaney, M. J. (2010). Epigenetics and the biological definition of gene x environment interactions. *Child Development, 81*, 41–79.

O'Connor, T. G., & Croft, C. M. (2001). A twin study of attachment in preschool children. *Child Development, 72*, 1501–1511.

Picardi, A., Fagnani, C., Nisticò, L., & Stazi, M. A. (2011). A twin study of attachment style in young adults. *Journal of Personality, 79*, 965–992.

Pinquart, M., Feußner, C., & Ahnert, L. (2013). Meta-analytic evidence for stability in attachments from infancy to early adulthood. *Attachment and Human Development, 15*, 189–218.

Roisman, G. I., & Fraley, R. C. (2008). A behavior–genetic study of parenting quality, infant attachment security, and their covariation in a nationally representative sample. *Developmental Psychology, 44*, 831–839.

Simpson, J., & Belsky, J. (2008). Attachment theory within a modern evolutionary framework. In J. Cassidy & P. Shaver (Eds.), *Handbook of attachment: Theory, research, and clinical applications* (2nd ed., pp. 131–158). New York, NY: Guilford Press.

Sroufe, L. A., Bennett, C., Englund, M., Urban, J., & Shulman, S. (1993). The significance of gender boundaries in preadolescence: Contemporary correlates and antecedents of boundary violation and maintenance. *Child Development, 64*, 455–466.

Torgersen, A. M., Grova, B. K., & Sommerstad, R. (2007). A pilot study of attachment patterns in adult twins. *Attachment and Human Development, 9*, 127–138.

Toth, I., Lakatos, K., & Gervai, J. (2013). Gender differences in children's responses to attachment story stems: True or artefacts? *Bulletin of the International Society for the Study of Behavioural Development, 63*, 2–5.

Venta, A., Shmueli-Goetz, Y., & Sharp, C. (2014). Assessing attachment in adolescence: A psychometric study of the child attachment interview. *Psychological Assessment, 26*, 238–255.

Ventura, T., Gomes, M. C., Pita, A., Neto, M. T., & Taylor, A. (2013). Digit ratio (2D:4D) in newborns: Influences of prenatal testosterone and maternal environment. *Early Human Development, 89*, 107–112.

Walker, R., Burger, O., Wagner, J., & Von Rueden, C. R. (2006). Evolution of brain size and juvenile periods in primates. *Journal of Human Evolution, 51*, 480–489.

Weisner, T. S. (1996). The 5–7 transition as an ecocultural project. In A. Sameroff & M. Haith (Eds.), *The five to seven year shift: The age of reason and responsibility* (pp. 295–326). Chicago, IL: University of Chicago Press.

West-Eberhard, M. J. (2003). *Developmental plasticity and evolution.* New York, NY: Oxford University Press.

MARCO DEL GIUDICE is an assistant professor in the Department of Psychology at the University of New Mexico, Albuquerque, NM, USA.

Brumariu, L. E. (2015). Parent–child attachment and emotion regulation. In G. Bosmans &
K. A. Kerns (Eds.), *Attachment in middle childhood: Theoretical advances and new directions
in an emerging field. New Directions for Child and Adolescent Development, 148*, 31–45.

3

Parent–Child Attachment and Emotion Regulation

Laura E. Brumariu

Abstract

*Given the centrality of both parent–child attachment and emotion regulation
in children's development and adjustment, it is important to evaluate the relations between these constructs. This article discusses conceptual and empirical
links between attachment and emotion regulation in middle childhood, highlights progress and challenges in the literature, and outlines future inquiries.
Studies have established that securely attached children internalize effective
emotion regulation strategies within the attachment relationship and are able
to successfully employ adaptive emotion regulation strategies outside the attachment relationship, when the attachment figure is not present. There are not
enough studies to conclude yet that the insecure attachment patterns (ambivalent, avoidant, and disorganized) may relate differentially with emotion regulation processes. Studies investigating whether there are unique links between
the four attachment patterns and the various emotion regulation processes will
advance the field considerably. Studies evaluating the associations between attachment and emotion regulation will benefit from a multimethod approach in
measuring these constructs. Embedding the relation between parent–child attachment and emotion regulation within broader developmental models will further advance the research on this topic. © 2015 Wiley Periodicals, Inc.*

A ttachment theory provides one of the most comprehensive frameworks for understanding social and emotional development. Bowlby (1969, 1973) postulated that the quality of parent–child relationships sets the foundation for later personality development and that a secure attachment relationship maps onto healthy adaptation, whereas insecure attachments signal a risk for difficulties in later functioning and potential clinical symptoms. Advances in research since the development of the attachment theory over half a century ago have demonstrated that the quality of parent–child attachment is one of the key environmental determinants or correlates of children's well-being. For example, securely attached children experience fewer internalizing and externalizing difficulties (Brumariu & Kerns, 2010; Fearon, Bakermans-Kranenburg, van Ijzendoorn, Lapsley, & Roisman, 2010; Moss & Lecompte, Article 5, this issue), are more socially competent, and have better friendship quality (Pallini, Baiocco, Schneider, Madigan, & Atkinson, 2014).

Another construct that has received increasing attention in the past two to three decades is emotion regulation. Literature has shown that aspects of emotion regulation are associated with positive developmental outcomes (e.g., social competence; Contreras & Kerns, 2000) and play a critical role in clinical conditions (e.g., externalizing problems, anxiety; Brumariu, Kerns, & Seibert, 2012; Mullin & Hinshaw, 2007). Given the significance of both parent–child attachment and emotion regulation in children's healthy development and maladjustment, it is essential to deepen our understanding of their relation in middle childhood.

After receiving little attention for many years, with "a great deal … left to imagination" (Waters & Cummings, 2000, p. 166), attachment in middle childhood is now recognized as a key phase in human development. While attachment figures continue to function both as *safe havens* in time of distress and as *secure bases* that support a child's exploration, there is a shift in middle childhood toward greater co-regulation of secure base contact between the child and parent figure, with the child taking increasingly more responsibility in coordinating with the attachment figure. Thus, the availability (rather than proximity) of an attachment figure is a primary characteristic of attachment at this age (Bowlby, 1988; see Bosmans & Kerns, Article 1, this issue). As children become more autonomous, their social world expands, and peer relationships become more important. Key developmental tasks include a growing need to self-regulate and rely on effective emotion regulation strategies. This article discusses conceptual and empirical links between attachment and emotion regulation in middle childhood, highlights progress and challenges in the literature, and suggests future inquiries. It is important to note that the studies reviewed here relied on a diversity of questionnaires, interviews, and story stem tasks, which allows us to assess the attachment construct in middle childhood more thoroughly (Bosmans & Kerns, Article 1, this issue).

NEW DIRECTIONS FOR CHILD AND ADOLESCENT DEVELOPMENT • DOI: 10.1002/cad

Theoretical Links Between Parent–Child Attachment and Emotion Regulation

The attachment system has a safety-regulation function in that, if activated by negative emotionally provoking situations, it prompts the child to seek support from the parent. Attachment is not, however, only an emergency response system. Children's ability to use an attachment figure as a secure base also provides the self-regulatory capacities necessary to explore and master everyday situations (Waters & Cummings, 2000). From this perspective, parents' roles are those of "external organizers" (Zimmermann, Maier, Winter, & Grossmann, 2001), and parent–child relationships offer a meaningful context for emotion socialization, the product of which are emotion regulation abilities. Children learn about emotion and emotion regulation strategies in the interaction with their caregivers through a variety of socialization methods, such as directly being taught and communicating about their emotions and ways they are helped to modulate their emotional responses. It is likely that children also learn by observing attachment figures' expression of their own emotions and regulation abilities (Denham, Bassett, & Wyatt, 2010). The emerging (yet limited) parenting literature in middle childhood provides initial evidence that parenting strategies and emotion socialization practices are related to parent–child attachment. For example, mothers of securely attached children tend to adopt an emotion coaching (rather than a dismissing) meta-emotion philosophy when discussing challenging emotions such as anger (Chen, Lin, & Li, 2012), express less negative emotion when talking about their child, and show less directly observed anger when discussing a challenging topic with their child (Scott, Riskman, Woolgar, Humayun, & O'Connor, 2011).

Attachment theorists (e.g., Cassidy, 1994; Thompson & Meyer, 2007) proposed that differences in parent–child attachment organization are particularly important for the development of emotion regulation, which suggests that children with secure and insecure attachments should rely on different emotion regulation strategies. By definition, it is expected that securely attached children, through repeated interactions with caregivers who are sensitive, flexible, and encourage a range of emotions, are able to openly express their emotions, learn (within the attachment relationship) effective ways to manage negative emotions in stressful situations, are able to alleviate their distress, and return to exploration of the environment (Contreras & Kerns, 2000). In a seminal paper, Cassidy (1994) described differences in emotion regulation characteristics of insecurely attached children *within* the attachment relationship, based on infant studies (see also Sroufe, 1983). These emotion regulation strategies are evolutionarily adaptive as they prepare children to cope with different types of rearing environments (Simpson & Belsky, 2008). Specifically, ambivalently attached children heighten their display of negative emotions, ostensibly in an effort to gain the attention of their inconsistently available attachment figure. Avoidantly attached children minimize their negative emotions when interacting with their attachment figure, which permits them to maintain a relationship with an attachment figure who cannot tolerate attachment behaviors. Children with disorganized attachments miss opportunities to learn how to mitigate their distress and develop developmentally appropriate emotion regulation strategies (Lyons-Ruth & Jacobvitz, 2008) as they cope with caregivers' alternating patterns of hostile/intrusive behavior, role-reversing, misattuned affect, and/or detachment (Madigan et al., 2006). Similarly, influences of attachment on emotion regulation strategies are expected in middle childhood; however, by this age, children should be able to apply their emotion regulation abilities *outside* the parent–child dyad and carry them forward in social settings. Further, the repertoire of emotion regulation strategies becomes more sophisticated at this age. Noteworthy markers of emotional development in middle childhood include awareness of multiple complex emotions, awareness of emotion "scripts" in social situations, and use of expressive behavior to maintain relationship dynamics (e.g., smiling in social settings; Saarni, 1999).

A major challenge in testing the assumption that differences in attachment organization are associated with different emotion regulation strategies, with the securely attached children displaying better emotion regulation, has been a lack of shared, integrative set of definitions of emotion regulation. As a fairly recent concept, emotion regulation is a broad construct that has been defined in many ways. For example, Shields and Cicchetti (1997) defined emotion regulation as reflecting differences in lability, flexibility, and situational responsivity that lead to adaptive functioning and appropriate emotional expression in emotionally arousing situations. Other definitions emphasize the heterogeneous set of processes involved in regulating one's emotions, and some include emotion reactivity. As such, emotion regulation has been defined as reflecting modulating and changing emotional states, managing emotion responding and modulating behavioral expression of emotions (Eisenberg & Spinrad, 2004), differences in emotions as regulating and as regulated (Cole, Martin, & Dennis, 2004), or "monitoring, evaluating, and modifying emotional reactions, especially their intensive and temporal features, to accomplish one's goal" (Thompson & Meyer, 2007, p. 251). In spite of the lack of a consensual definition, most conceptualizations of emotion regulation point out that successful management and modulation of emotional experiences across time and across situations to accomplish a specific goal are important emotion regulation abilities. To evaluate whether security of attachment is linked with better emotion regulation strategies and whether there are differences in emotion regulation among the insecure attachment patterns (ambivalent, avoidant, and disorganized), the studies discussed in this article are organized in four categories: monitoring and understanding emotional states, emotional experiences and expressions, ways of regulating emotions (i.e., coping), and overall emotion regulation.

NEW DIRECTIONS FOR CHILD AND ADOLESCENT DEVELOPMENT • DOI: 10.1002/cad

It is also important to keep in mind that emotion regulation and emotional competence are two related and overlapping constructs, and it might be challenging to tease them apart conceptually and methodologically. Saarni (1999) suggested that emotional competence entails self-efficacy in emotion-eliciting transactions and encompasses emotion-related capacities and abilities that an individual needs to function in a changing environment so that he or she emerges as more differentiated, better adapted, effective, and confident. I see emotion regulation capacities as necessary prerequisites for reaching emotion competence. Nonetheless, terms such as "emotion understanding" most likely reflect both emotion regulation and emotional competence.

Empirical Links Between Attachment and Emotion Regulation

This section describes empirical links between attachment and four aspects of emotion regulation: emotion understanding, emotional experiences and expressions, ways of regulating emotions, and overall emotion regulation.

Attachment and Emotion Understanding. The term "emotion understanding" refers both to monitoring/awareness of one's emotional states and to discerning/understanding others' emotional expressions (e.g., recognizing, appraising, and labeling other's feelings). Only three studies addressed the topic of the relations between attachment and emotion understanding in middle childhood. Findings suggest that, as expected, securely attached children report greater emotional awareness (Brumariu et al., 2012), are better at identifying and labeling emotions (Steele, Steele, & Croft, 2008), and have better knowledge of emotion regulation strategies, such as cognitive engagement, than insecurely attached children (Colle & Del Giudice, 2011).

Whereas one can speculate that disorganized children might develop good emotion recognition abilities to serve them in coping with an overwhelming and unpredictable caregiver, the hypothesis that disorganized children may miss opportunities to develop this emotion regulation ability due to a chaotic emotion-related environment is also plausible. Studies show that children with disorganized attachment in particular are at a disadvantage in their ability to monitor their own emotions and access knowledge of emotion regulation strategies (Brumariu et al., 2012; Colle & Del Giudice, 2011). However, results are mixed regarding their ability to discriminate among emotions. In one study, children with a history of attachment disorganization in infancy were not different in their emotion recognition abilities than children with a history of security (Steele et al., 2008). In another study, however, among all attachment patterns, based on a story stem task, disorganized children aged 7 years scored lower on nonverbal discrimination of both relatively easy (e.g., joy) and complex (e.g., anxiety) emotions (matching the target emotion with the correct one in brief movie clips; Colle & Del Giudice, 2011). In addition, they tended to have lower emotion labeling scores. Further, ambivalent and avoidant children produced the highest proportion of behavioral engagement strategies (e.g., modifying the situation) and fewer behavioral diversion strategies (e.g., displaying attention away from the triggering situation) when asked what a person in a picture can do to feel differently (Colle & Del Giudice, 2011). Importantly, the deficits (and skills) in labeling emotions of avoidant and ambivalent children may serve them well in maintaining the attachment relationship. For example, Steele et al. (2008) reported that avoidantly attached children are particularly skilled at recognizing happy faces, perhaps because displaying positive mood may facilitate interaction with their attachment figure; they had difficulty labeling the facial emotions of mischief and surprise, as did children with ambivalent attachment. Ambivalent children had also difficulty identifying happy faces correctly, which may reflect difficulties with positive emotional exchanges (see Steele at al., 2008).

Attachment and Emotional Experiences and Expressions. Several studies assessed relations of attachment with modulation of emotions *within* the parent–child relationship. More securely attached girls showed higher levels of observed overall positivity and lower levels of embarrassment in a parent–child interaction task asking the dyads to tell each other what they like most about each other (Hershenberg et al., 2011). Interestingly, self-reported preoccupied, dismissive, and fearful attachments, but not secure attachment, were related to Taiwanese children ratings of their negative emotional reactions to a recent mother–child conflict (Liu & Huang, 2012). In a study by Spangler and Zimmermann (2014), 12-year-olds and their mothers participated in two interaction tasks designed to induce negative emotions (anger and fear). The interaction tasks were later coded for facial and verbal expressions. Children and mothers reported on children's emotions during the tasks. Children classified as secure in infancy reported more intense anger (but not fear) than the insecurely attached children, and their ratings of emotions in both tasks were similar to their mothers' ratings. These findings support the idea that securely attached children are able to coregulate distress within the attachment relationship (but see Liu & Huang, 2012, for nonsignificant findings). They feel free to experience emotional states and express both positive and negative emotions openly, and secure mother–child dyads are in sync regarding children's emotional experiences. When comparing disorganized and nondisorganized children, no differences in emotional expression were found (Spangler & Zimmermann, 2014). Emotional experience may be difficult to report or express, particularly in children with disorganized attachment. Nonetheless, it can be inferred by relying on physiological markers associated with emotion regulation (Gunnar, Talge, & Herrera, 2009). Children with a disorganized attachment in the Spangler and Zimmermann study showed an increase in cortisol levels, a biomarker of stress, following the interaction task.

An additional set of studies examined the relation of attachment with management of emotional experiences *outside* the attachment relationship, in everyday situations. Studies showed that girls with more secure attachment experience more positive and less negative emotions rated over 2 weeks (Abraham & Kerns, 2013) and that securely attached children, based on a story stem interview or questionnaire, report more positive daily mood and less negative daily mood (Kerns, Abraham, Schlegelmilch & Morgan, 2007). In Kerns et al.'s (2007) study of 9- to 11-year-olds, children classified as disorganized or ambivalent on the interview reported more negative mood than children classified as secure; however, avoidant and secure children were no different from each other. Further, securely attached children showed better frustration tolerance in the classroom based on their teachers' reports.

Two additional studies investigated the link between attachment security and children's management of global emotional intensity in late middle childhood. Contreras, Kerns, Weimer, Gentzler, and Tomich (2000) found no relation between an attachment composite score, based on a semistructured interview and the Security Scale (SS; Kerns, Aspelmeier, Gentzler, & Grabill, 2001) and mother-reported negative affectivity. By contrast, Brumariu and Kerns (2013) found that children with a history of more attachment security in infancy were rated by their parents as being more capable of managing intense emotions. Children with a more disorganized attachment history showed poorer ability to manage intense emotions based on father reports but not based on mother reports.

Some studies assessed the association of attachment and interpreting and managing emotions *in emotionally challenging or threatening situations*. Brumariu et al. (2012) found that more securely attached children tended to express lower levels of catastrophizing (always expecting the worst to happen) and personalizing (taking responsibility for negative outcomes), whereas children with more disorganized attachment representations reported higher levels of catastrophizing when evaluating hypothetical, challenging situations. More securely attached children based on the SS indicated that they would (appropriately) feel angry, sad, and scared in response to watching marital conflict videos, after receiving instructions to imagine that the actors in the videos were their parents (Harold, Shelton, Goeke-Morey, & Cummings, 2004). Further, Borelli et al. (2010) investigated children's positive and negative emotions and cortisol levels in a fear-startle paradigm before and after the administration of an attachment interview with children aged 8 to 12 years. Higher narrative coherence (i.e., security) was related to greater self-reported positive emotions, but not with negative emotions measured before an attachment interview. More securely attached children showed a steeper increase in reports of positive affect during an attachment interview and a steeper decline in negative affect from before to after fear-induced startle. Findings regarding associations of security with cortisol levels were mixed, and attachment security was unrelated to fear-potentiated startle. Compared to secure children, avoidant children reported less distress than their startle response and cortisol level indicated (Borelli, David, Crowley, Snavely, & Mayes, 2013; Borelli, West, Weekes, & Crowley, 2014).

Two additional studies relied on physiological markers of emotion regulation. Gilissen, Bakermans-Kranenburg, van Ijzendoorn, and Linting (2008) assessed attachment in 7-year-olds with a story stem task and the amount of stress (electrodermal activity) during stress-evoking episodes of the Trier Social Stress Test for Children (TSST-C). Children with insecure attachments, compared with their secure counterparts, showed higher levels of stress. They also responded with less skin conductance reactivity, although not with decreased heart rate variability in response to a fear-inducing film clip (Gilissen, Bakermans-Kranenburg, van Ijzendoorn, & van der Veer, 2008). Studies also evaluated neural responses during a virtual ball game with unfamiliar peers that included fair play, exclusion, and reunion. Dismissal/avoidance and self-reported distress were not related, but dismissal predicted frontal slow-wave event-related potentials (ERPs) during rejection and underreporting of distress relative to ERPs (White et al., 2012). Compared to secure children, avoidant children showed a greater increase in N2—a neural marker of expectancy violations—during reunion (White, Wu, Borelli, Mayes, & Crowley, 2013). These findings provide initial evidence for a positivity bias of avoidantly attached children and suggest that emotion regulation strategies characteristic of attachment classifications may translate to similar strategies used in social contexts.

Collectively, although there are some inconsistent findings, the literature regarding middle childhood indicates that more securely attached children show more positive emotions when interacting with their attachment caregiver, experience more positive and less negative mood states outside the attachment relationship, and are better at interpreting and modulating emotions in emotionally challenging situations. Although the literature is very limited, findings suggest that disorganized children experience more negative mood, have poorer ability to manage intense emotions, and experience stress more intensely in interactions with their attachment figure. Little is known about the abilities of ambivalent and avoidant children to modulate emotional experiences, though emerging evidence suggests a positive bias related to avoidance.

Attachment and Ways of Regulating Emotions. Several studies showed that in later middle childhood, more securely attached children use constructive coping strategies when dealing with distress based on mothers' reports of coping (Contreras et al., 2000; Kerns et al., 2007) or children's reports of coping (Bauminger & Kimhi-Kind, 2008). However, attachment classifications based on a story stem task were not related to coping (Kerns et al., 2007). Other studies evaluated whether attachment is related to the use of specific coping strategies. Findings suggest that more securely attached children use more social-support coping and problem-solving coping (Abraham & Kerns, 2013). Also, one year later, secure children showed greater use of support-seeking coping, avoidant coping, and distraction coping (Gaylord-Harden, Taylor, Campbell, Kesselring, & Grant, 2009). Attachment predicted active coping for boys but not for girls. Similarly, Liu and Huang (2012) reported that Taiwanese children with secure, dismissive, or preoccupied attachments rely more on approach coping strategies, whereas fearful adolescents use this strategy less. In addition, secure and dismissing adolescents engaged in more distancing coping. Thus, coping skills (and other emotion regulation aspects) are not inherently optimal or maladaptive, and they may be appropriate depending on the individual's goal for the situation (Thompson & Meyer, 2007), which is very likely to be influenced by cultural norms. For example, distancing might be an effective strategy when distancing from conflict is a sign of respect (Liu & Huang, 2012). Regarding insecure organized attachment patterns, Brenning, Soenens, Braet, and Bosmans (2012) found that children with avoidant or anxious attachments use higher dysregulation and suppression of negative emotions. However, anxious attachment was associated with dysregulation primarily and avoidant attachment was uniquely associated with suppression when controlling for the variance shared between anxiety and avoidance. Regarding attachment disorganization, Brumariu et al. (2012) showed that children with more disorganized attachment representations were rated by their mothers as using lower levels of active coping strategies (problem-focused and positive restructuring).

Two studies investigated associations between attachment and coping strategies used to regulate discrete emotions. More securely attached children use more constructive strategies to regulate anger (Schwarz, Stutz, & Ledermann, 2012). Further, children with more avoidant attachments employ anger dysregulation and sadness suppression, whereas children with more anxious attachments rely on both anger and sadness dysregulation (Brenning & Braet, 2013). Taken together, these findings confirm that securely attached children employ effective coping strategies in different contexts, depending on what is adaptive in a specific context. It is less clear if there are pronounced differences in the use of specific coping skills by children with insecure attachment patterns.

Attachment and Overall Emotion Regulation. Some studies assessed emotion regulation as a broad construct in addition to or rather than evaluating specific aspects of emotion regulation. Findings show that attachment security is linked to lower levels of observer-rated emotion dysregulation, such as tearful and dramatic affect, within the parent–child dyad (Hershenberg et al., 2011) and that when interacting with their mothers in two challenging tasks, securely attached children use social emotion regulation strategies (e.g., negative emotions were communicated directly toward the mother; Spangler & Zimmermann, 2014). Narrative coherence or security, measured either with an interview or a questionnaire, was not related to parent reports of emotion regulation (Borelli et al., 2010; Kim & Page, 2013).

Conclusions and Future Directions

There has been substantial progress in characterizing the relation between parent–child attachment security and emotion regulation in middle childhood. Studies have established that securely attached children internalize effective emotion regulation strategies within the attachment relationship and are able to employ adaptive emotion regulation strategies outside the attachment relationship, when the attachment figure is not present. Consistent with the tenets that secure children utilize their attachment figures as *safe havens* and *secure bases*, there is evidence that secure children use effective emotion regulation strategies in both challenging and ordinary environments.

Fewer studies tested the links of insecure attachment patterns with emotion regulation, and there are not enough accrued data to conclude that specific forms of insecure attachment (e.g., ambivalence) are associated with distinct emotion profiles, as Cassidy (1994) and Sroufe (1983) have suggested (but see, e.g., Borelli et al., 2010; Brenning et al., 2012; Brumariu & Kerns, 2013; Brumariu et al., 2012). Initial findings, however, suggest that the insecure attachment patterns might relate differentially with emotion regulation processes, although most evidence refers to disorganized attachment. Studies investigating whether there are unique links between all four attachment patterns and various emotion regulation processes will advance the field considerably.

The measurement of both attachment and emotion regulation expanded substantially in the last two decades (see Bosmans & Kerns, Article 1, this issue). A multimethod approach to measuring attachment will provide a richer understanding of the links between attachment and emotion regulation. Further, most studies focused on traitlike aspects of emotion regulation (e.g., positive mood), and few studies assessed emotion regulation in real time or employed physiological or neural markers in addition to behavioral indicators of emotion regulation (for exceptions, see Borelli et al., 2010, 2013; Gilissen, Bakermans-Kranenburg, van Ijzendoorn, & Linting, 2008; Gilissen, Bakermans-Kranenburg, van Ijzendoorn, & van der Veer, 2008; White et al., 2012, 2013). Multimethod assessments capturing subjective, biological, and behavioral facets of emotion regulation, investigation of discrete complex emotions, and inclusion of experimental designs, accompanied by interviews in which the child's goals are clear and emotion regulation strategies can be assessed in relation to this goal would enhance our understanding of how attachment and emotion regulation are related (Thompson & Meyer, 2007). In addition, the field would benefit considerably from studies taking a more nuanced developmental approach in conceptualizing emotion regulation (e.g., assessing regulation of conscious emotions in 6- to 7-year-olds and awareness of multiple emotions in 7- to 10-year-olds, Saarni, 1999; considering that various neural systems implicated in emotion regulation become effective or continue to mature at different time points in development, Thompson, Lewis, & Calkins, 2008). Studies with younger children relied on mild stressor paradigms to evaluate (among others) physiological markers of emotion regulation. A caveat to keep in mind is that with increasing age and increased emotion regulation abilities, it becomes difficult to design ethically acceptable (stress) paradigms that will allow the evaluation of physiological markers of emotion regulation, and that tasks that threaten the social self seem most successful (Gunnar et al., 2009). Reliance on diverse and at-risk samples will add to the literature, and more longitudinal studies will allow the disentangling of potential bidirectional effects.

Current work highlights several additional exciting lines of inquiry. Del Giudice (2009; Article 2, this issue) advanced the idea that due in part to biological changes, gender differences in attachment may emerge during middle childhood, with girls tending toward ambivalence and boys tending toward avoidance (see Bakermans-Kranenburg & van Ijzendoorn, 2009, for mixed evidence). Further, parents may encourage different emotion strategies for boys and girls. Studies showed that in spite of similarities, there are some differences in fathers' and mothers' emotion socialization approaches (Brand & Klimes-Dougan, 2010). For example, mothers provide more opportunities for emotion understanding, while children's interactions with fathers are characterized by more emotional arousal. Fathers have been rarely included in research, and it would be important to investigate whether the relation between attachment and emotion regulation depends on the gender of the child and of the attachment figure (see Gaylord-Harden et al., 2009).

A small number of studies assessed factors that influence the relation between attachment and emotion regulation. Gilissen, Bakermans-Kranenburg, van Ijzendoorn, and Linting (2008) demonstrated an interaction effect of attachment security and 5-HTTLPR, a genetic polymorphism associated with stress, on electrodermal reactivity during a stressful task. Children with two long alleles and a secure attachment showed the lowest levels of stress. Further, temperamentally more fearful children with less secure relationships showed the highest skin conductance reactivity during a fear-inducing procedure, whereas temperamentally fearful children with more secure relationships showed the lowest skin conductance (Gilissen, Bakermans-Kranenburg, van Ijzendoorn, & van der Veer, 2008). In another study, the effect of attachment disorganization on children's cortisol levels was stronger when children were feeling highly afraid in a negative emotion-eliciting task (Spangler & Zimmermann, 2014). Replicating and extending these findings by exploring the relation of attachment in combination with other social influences (e.g., peers), temperament, and genetics are an important next step. Emerging evidence suggests that emotion regulation processes may explain how attachment relates to child adjustment, including peer competence (Contreras et al., 2000), friendship (Schwarz et al., 2012), anxiety (Brumariu at al., 2012), depressive symptoms (Brenning et al., 2012), and externalizing problems (Brenning & Braet, 2013). An interesting question to be answered is whether specific aspects of emotion regulation mediate associations between attachment and other aspects of functioning (e.g., school adaptation). Another question is whether emotion regulation strategies internalized within attachment relationships would be generalized to other close or unfamiliar individuals. Embedding the relation between parent–child attachment and emotion regulation within broader developmental models that include multiple influences will further advance the research on this topic.

References

Abraham, M., & Kerns, K. (2013). Positive and negative emotions and coping as mediators of mother–child attachment and peer relationships. *Merrill-Palmer Quarterly*, 59(4), 399–425. doi:10.1353/mpq.2013.0023

Bakermans-Kranenburg, M. J., & van Ijzendoorn, M. H. (2009). No reliable gender differences in attachment across the lifespan. *Behavioral and Brain Sciences*, 32(1), 22–23. doi.org/10.1017/S0140525X0900003X

Bauminger, N., & Kimhi-Kind, I. (2008). Social information processing, security of attachment, and emotion regulation in children with learning disabilities. *Journal of Learning Disabilities*, 41(4), 315–332. doi:10.1177/0022219408316095

Borelli, J., Crowley, M., David, D., Sbarra, D., Anderson, G., & Mayes, L. (2010). Attachment and emotion in school-aged children. *Emotion*, 10(4), 475–485. doi:10.1037/a0018490

Borelli, J., David, D., Crowley, M., Snavely, J., & Mayes, L. (2013). Dismissing children's perceptions of their emotional experience and parental care: Preliminary evidence of positive bias. *Child Psychiatry & Human Development*, 44(1), 70–88. doi:10.1007/s10578-012-0310-5

Borelli, J. L., West, J. L., Weekes, N. Y., & Crowley, M. J. (2014). Dismissing child attachment and discordance for subjective and neuroendocrine responses to vulnerability. *Developmental Psychobiology*, 56(3), 584–591. doi:10.1002/dev.21107

Bowlby, J. (1969). *Attachment and loss: Vol. 1. Attachment*. New York, NY: Basic Books.

Bowlby, J. (1973). *Attachment and loss: Vol. 2. Separation: Anxiety and anger*. New York, NY: Basic Books.

Bowlby, J. (1988). *A secure base: Parent–child attachment and healthy human development*. New York, NY: Basic Books.

Brand, A. E., & Klimes-Dougan, B. (2010). Emotion socialization in adolescence: The roles of mothers and fathers. In A. Kennedy Root & S. Denham (Eds.), *New Directions for Child and Adolescent Development: No. 128. The role of gender in the socialization of emotion: Key concepts and critical issues* (pp. 85–100). San Francisco, CA: Jossey-Bass.

Brenning, K. M., & Braet, C. (2013). The emotion regulation model of attachment: An emotion-specific approach. *Personal Relationships*, 20(1), 107–123. doi:10.1111/j.1475-6811.2012.01399.x

Brenning, K. M., Soenens, B., Braet, C., & Bosmans, G. (2012). Attachment and depressive symptoms in middle childhood and early adolescence: Testing the validity of the emotion regulation model of attachment. *Personal Relationships*, 19, 445–464. doi:10.1111/j.1475-6811.2011.01372.x

Brumariu, L. E., & Kerns, K. A. (2010). Parent–child attachment and internalizing symptoms in childhood and adolescence: A review of empirical findings and future directions. *Development and Psychopathology, 22*(1), 177–203. doi:10.1017/S0954579409990344

Brumariu, L. E., & Kerns, K. A. (2013). Pathways to anxiety: Contributions of attachment history, temperament, peer competence, and ability to manage intense emotions. *Child Psychiatry and Human Development, 44*, 504–515. doi:10.1007/s10578-012-0345-7

Brumariu, L. E., Kerns, K. A., & Seibert, A. C. (2012). Mother–child attachment, emotion regulation, and anxiety symptoms in middle childhood. *Personal Relationships, 19*, 569–585. doi:10.1111/j.1475-6811.2011.01379.x

Cassidy, J. (1994). Emotion regulation: Influences on attachment relationships. In N. A. Fox (Ed.), *The development of emotion regulation: Biological and behavioral considerations. Monographs of the Society for Research in Child Development, 59* (Serial No. 240), 228–249. doi:10.1111/j.1540-5834.1994.tb01287.x

Chen, F., Lin, H., & Li, C. (2012). The role of emotion in parent–child relationships: Children's emotionality, maternal meta-emotion, and children's attachment security. *Journal of Child and Family Studies, 21*(3), 403–410. doi:10.1007/s10826-011-9491-y

Cole, P. M., Martin, S. E., & Dennis, T. A. (2004). Emotion regulation as a scientific construct: Methodological challenges and directions for child development research. *Child Development, 75*(2), 317–333. doi:10.1111/j.1467-8624.2004.00673.x

Colle, L., & Del Giudice, M. (2011). Patterns of attachment and emotional competence in middle childhood. *Social Development, 20*(1), 51–72. doi:10.1111/j.1467-9507.2010.00576.x

Contreras, J. M., & Kerns, K. A. (2000). Emotion regulation processes: Explaining links between parent-child attachment and peer relationships. In K. A. Kerns, J. M. Contreras, and A. M. Neal-Barnett (Eds.), *Family and peers: Linking two social worlds* (pp. 1–25). Westport, CT: Praeger.

Contreras, J. M., Kerns, K. A., Weimer, B. L., Gentzler, A. L., & Tomich, P. L. (2000). Emotion regulation as a mediator of associations between mother–child attachment and peer relationships in middle childhood. *Journal of Family Psychology, 14*, 111–124. doi:10.1037/0893-3200.14.1.111

Del Giudice, M. (2009). Sex, attachment, and the development of reproductive strategies. *Behavioral and Brain Sciences, 32*(1), 1–21.

Denham, S. A., Bassett, H. H., & Wyatt, T. M. (2010). Gender differences in the socialization of preschoolers' emotional competence. In A. Kennedy Root & S. Denham (Eds.), *New Directions for Child and Adolescent Development: No. 128. The role of gender in the socialization of emotion: Key concepts and critical issues* (pp. 29–49). San Francisco, CA: Jossey-Bass.

Eisenberg, N., & Spinrad, T. L. (2004). Emotion-related regulation: Sharpening the definition. *Child Development, 75*, 334–339. doi:10.1111/j.1467-8624.2004.00674.x

Fearon, R. P., Bakermans-Kranenburg, M. J., van Ijzendoorn, M. H., Lapsley, A., & Roisman, G. I. (2010). The significance of insecure attachment and disorganization in the development of children's externalizing behavior: A meta-analytic study. *Child Development, 81*(2), 435–456. doi:10.1111/j.1467-8624.2009.01405.x

Gaylord-Harden, N., Taylor, J., Campbell, C., Kesselring, C., & Grant, K. (2009). Maternal attachment and depressive symptoms in urban adolescents: The influence of coping strategies and gender. *Journal of Clinical Child and Adolescent Psychology, 38*(5), 684–695. doi:10.1080/15374410903103569

Gilissen, R., Bakermans-Kranenburg, M., van Ijzendoorn, M., & Linting, M. (2008). Electrodermal reactivity during the trier social stress test for children: Interaction between the serotonin transporter polymorphism and children's attachment representation. *Developmental Psychobiology, 50*(6), 615–625. doi:10.1002/dev.20314

Gilissen, R., Bakermans-Kranenburg, M., van Ijzendoorn, M., & van der Veer, R. (2008). Parent–child relationship, temperament, and physiological reactions to fear-inducing film clips: Further evidence for differential susceptibility. *Journal of Experimental Child Psychology, 99*, 182–195. doi:10.1016/j.jecp.2007.06.004

Gunnar, M. R., Talge, N. M., & Herrera, A. (2009). Stressor paradigms in developmental studies: What does and does not work to produce mean increases in salivary cortisol. *Psychoneuroendocrinology, 34*(7), 953–967.

Harold, G., Shelton, K., Goeke-Morey, M., & Cummings, E. M. (2004). Marital conflict, child emotional security about family relationships and child adjustment. *Social Development, 13*(3), 350–376. doi:10.1111/j.1467-9507.2004.00272.x

Hershenberg, R., Davila, J., Yoneda, A., Starr, L., Miller, M., Stroud, C., & Feinstein, B. (2011). What I like about you: The association between adolescent attachment security and emotional behavior in a relationship promoting context. *Journal of Adolescence, 34*, 1017–1024. doi:10.1016/j.adolescence.2010.11.006

Kerns, K. A., Abraham, M., Schlegelmilch, A., & Morgan, T. (2007). Mother–child attachment in later middle childhood: Assessment approaches and associations with mood and emotion regulation. *Attachment and Human Development, 9*(1), 33–53. doi:10.1080/1461673060115144

Kerns, K. A., Aspelmeier, J. E., Gentzler, A. L., & Grabill, C. M. (2001). Parent–child attachment and monitoring in middle childhood. *Journal of Family Psychology, 15*, 69–81. doi:10.1037//0893-3200.15.1.69

Kim, H., & Page, T. (2013). Emotional bonds with parents, emotion regulation, and school-related behavior problems among elementary school truants. *Journal of Child and Family Studies, 22*, 869–878. doi:10.1007/s10826-012-9646-5

Liu, Y.-L., & Huang, F.-M. (2012). Mother–adolescent conflict in Taiwan: Links between attachment style and psychological distress. *Social Behavior and Personality, 40*(6), 919–932. doi:10.2224/sbp.2012.40.6.919

Lyons-Ruth, K., & Jacobvitz, D. (2008). Attachment disorganization: Genetic factors, parenting contexts, and developmental transformation from infancy to adulthood. In J. Cassidy & P. Shaver (Eds.), *Handbook of attachment* (2nd ed., pp. 666–697). New York, NY: Guilford Press.

Madigan, S., Bakermans-Kranenburg, M. J., van Ijzendoorn, M. H., Moran, G., Pederson, D. R., & Benoit, D. (2006). Unresolved states of mind, anomalous parental behavior, and disorganized attachment: A review and meta-analysis of a transmission gap. *Attachment & Human Development, 8*(2), 89–111. doi:10.1080/14616730600774458

Mullin, B. C., & Hinshaw, S. P. (2007). Emotion regulation and externalizing disorders in children and adolescents. In J. J. Gross (Ed.), *Handbook of emotion regulation* (pp. 523–541). New York, NY: Guilford Press.

Pallini, S., Baiocco, R., Schneider, B. H., Madigan, S., & Atkinson, L. (2014). Early child–parent attachment and peer relations: A meta-analysis of recent research. *Journal of Family Psychology, 28*(1), 118–123. doi:10.1037/a0035736

Saarni, C. (1999). *The development of emotional competence.* New York, NY: Guilford Press.

Schwarz, B., Stutz, M., & Ledermann, T. (2012). Perceived interparental conflict and early adolescents' friendships: The role of attachment security and emotion regulation. *Journal of Youth and Adolescence, 41*, 1240–1252. doi:10.1007/s10964-012-9769-4

Scott, S., Riskman, J., Woolgar, M., Humayun, S., & O'Connor, T. G. (2011). Attachment in adolescence: Overlap with parenting and unique prediction of behavioural adjustment. *Journal of Child Psychiatry and Psychology, 52*, 1052–1062. doi:10.1111/j.1469-7610.2011.02453.x

Shields, A., & Cicchetti, D. (1997). Emotion regulation among school-age children: The development and validation of a new criterion Q-sort scale. *Developmental Psychology, 6*, 906–916. doi:10.1037/0012-1649.33.6.906

Simpson, J. A., & Belsky, J. (2008). Attachment theory within a modern evolutionary framework. In J. Cassidy & P. Shaver (Eds.), *Handbook of attachment* (2nd ed., pp. 131–157). New York, NY: Guilford Press.

Spangler, G., & Zimmermann, P. (2014). Emotional and adrenocortical regulation in early adolescence: Prediction by attachment security and disorganization in infancy. *International Journal of Behavioral Development*, 38, 1–13. doi:10.1177/0165025414520808

Sroufe, L. A. (1983). Infant–caregiver attachment and patterns of adaptation in preschool: The roots of maladaptation and competence. In M. Perlmutter (Ed.), *Minnesota Symposium on Child Psychology: Vol. 16. Development and policy concerning children with special needs* (pp. 41–83). Hillsdale, NJ: Erlbaum.

Steele, H., Steele, M., & Croft, C. (2008). Early attachment predicts emotion recognition at 6 and 11 years old. *Attachment and Human Development*, 10(4), 379–393. doi:10.1080/14616730802461409

Thompson, R. A., Lewis, M. D., & Calkins, S. D. (2008). Reassessing emotion regulation. *Child Development Perspectives*, 2, 124–131. doi:10.1111/j.1750-8606.2008.00054.x

Thompson, R. A., & Meyer, S. (2007). Socialization of emotion regulation in the family. In J. J. Gross (Ed.), *Handbook of emotion regulation* (pp. 249–268). New York, NY: Guilford Press.

Waters, E., & Cummings, E. M. (2000). A secure base from which to explore close relationships. *Child Development*, 71(1), 164–172. doi:10.1111/1467-8624.00130

White, L. O., Wu, J., Borelli, J. L., Mayes, L. C., & Crowley, M. J. (2013). Play it again: Neural responses to reunion with excluders predicted by attachment patterns. *Developmental Science*, 16(6), 850–863. doi:10.1111/desc.12035

White, L. O., Wu, J., Borelli, J. L., Rutherford, H. J. V., David, D. H., Kim-Cohen, J., … Crowley, M. J. (2012). Attachment dismissal predicts frontal slow-wave ERPs during rejection by unfamiliar peers. *Emotion*, 12(4), 690–700. doi:10.1037/a0026750

Zimmermann, P., Maier, M., Winter, M., & Grossmann, K. (2001). Attachment and adolescents' emotion regulation during a joint problem-solving task with a friend. *International Journal of Behavioral Development*, 25(4), 331–343. doi:10.1080/01650250143000157

LAURA E. BRUMARIU is an assistant professor at the Gordon F. Derner Institute of Advanced Psychological Studies at Adelphi University.

NEW DIRECTIONS FOR CHILD AND ADOLESCENT DEVELOPMENT • DOI: 10.1002/cad

Zimmermann, P., & Iwanski, A. (2015). Attachment in middle childhood: Associations with information processing. In G. Bosmans & K. A. Kerns (Eds.), *Attachment in middle childhood: Theoretical advances and new directions in an emerging field. New Directions for Child and Adolescent Development, 148,* 47–61.

Attachment in Middle Childhood: Associations With Information Processing

Peter Zimmermann, Alexandra Iwanski

Abstract

Attachment theory suggests that internal working models of self and significant others influence adjustment during development by controlling information processing and self-regulation. We provide a conceptual overview on possible mechanisms linking attachment and information processing and review the current literature in middle childhood. Finally, we discuss and suggest future directions for research in this field. © 2015 Wiley Periodicals, Inc.

T here is ample evidence for caregiving influences on children's information processing in the field of emotional socialization (Eisenberg,
Cumberland, & Spinrad, 1998; Meyer, Raikes, Virmani, Waters, &
Thompson, 2014) and developmental psychopathology looking for effects
of deprivation or maltreatment (Belsky & de Haan, 2011; Colvert et al.,
2008; Pollak & Sinha, 2004). Attachment theory focuses specifically on
caregiving experiences in close emotional relationships and their influence
on social and emotional information processing across the life span, concur-
rently and longitudinally (Bowlby, 1980; Dykas & Cassidy, 2011). Bowlby
(1973) introduced the concept of internal working models (IWMs) of self
and others in attachment theory to provide a mechanism that explains
why and how attachment experiences are influential for information processing and self-regulation during development (Bretherton &
Munholland, 2008; Main, Kaplan, & Cassidy, 1985). Attachment theory has
inspired many researchers to study such processes. However, we know relatively little about the link between attachment and information processing
in middle childhood. In the first part of this article, we provide a theoretical
framework that illustrates possible links and mechanisms between attachment patterns and information processing using the concept of IWMs of
attachment. Then we review empirical evidence on the associations between attachment and different aspects of information processing. Finally,
we offer suggestions for future research perspectives in this field.

Attachment and Information Processing: The Functions of Internal Working Models

Information processing encompasses many different subprocesses such as
attention, perception, memory, pattern recognition, social evaluation, problem solving, decision making, and cognitive control (Massaro & Cowan,
1993). Crick and Dodge (1994) developed a model of social information
processing that excellently explains both aggression and depression. They
isolated (selective) encoding, (biased) interpretation, (restricted) goal clar-
ification, (restricted) problem solving, (restricted) response selection, and
(poor) strategy execution as relevant processes that all repeatedly access a
shared memory base. Lemerise and Arsenio (2000) added emotional components to this model. Bowlby (1973, 1980) had earlier explained similar
restricted social and emotional information processing as the effect of IWMs
of attachment that develop as a result of inappropriate caregiving, separations, threats of abandonment, or loss.

   Attachment and Internal Working Models. The attachment system
is a security regulation system (Bowlby, 1980) which is activated primarily in situations that elicit intense negative emotions that challenge or ex-
ceed the individual's self-regulation capacities (e.g., threats). Attachment
researchers therefore developed separation–reunion procedures that induce
age-appropriate distress and activate the attachment system (Ainsworth,

Blehar, Waters, & Wall, 1978; Main & Cassidy, 1988). Attachment patterns represent automatic patterns of emotion regulation (Cassidy, 1995; Spangler & Zimmermann, 2014; Zimmermann, Maier, Winter, & Grossmann, 2001). A secure attachment pattern functionally reflects an effective pattern of social emotion regulation in contact with the specific caregiver resulting in the child's confidence in exploring the environment again. In contrast, the insecure-avoidant attachment pattern reflects an ineffective individual emotion regulation, where the child tries to allocate attention to the environment (Main et al., 1985) but is not successful in downregulating distress (Spangler & Grossmann, 1993). The insecure-resistant attachment pattern reflects an ineffective social emotion regulation, as close contact to the caregiver is not downregulating the child's distress.

Attachment patterns are the result of the child's experiences of the caregiver's reactions when seeking proximity, comfort, or shelter (Ainsworth et al., 1978; Bowlby, 1980) or exploring the environment (Grossmann, Grossmann, Kindler, & Zimmermann, 2008; Waters & Cummings, 2000). Bowlby (1973) suggested that IWMs of self and caregiver control the attachment system and are generalized to social interactions outside the close relationship with attachment figures. Bowlby emphasized that IWMs serve optimal adjustment in the individual's environment when they are quite accurate constructions of the experienced social world. However, according to attachment theory, IWMs can be outdated, inappropriately generalized to other relationships or contexts, or cognitively disconnected when the child accepts the caregiver's interpretation of attachment-related experiences even when it contradicts the child's own experiences (Bretherton & Munholland, 2008). Thus, individuals may not consciously access or "know what they are not supposed to know," and do not access those feelings that they "are not supposed to feel" or express (Bowlby, 1988). Despite this restricted conscious access to own feelings, memories, and perceptions and the biased interpretation of other's reactions and intentions, a central assumption of attachment theory is that implicit, unconscious processes still control behavior and emotion regulation (Bowlby, 1980).

Structure of Internal Working Models. IWMs consist of an information processing component and an emotion regulation component that are in constant exchange and control the individual's self-regulation (Zimmermann, 1999; see Table 4.1). The information processing component influences attention, perception, memory, interpretation, and prediction of other's intentions and actions based on earlier attachment experiences. Perceptual processes include the allocation of attention to certain features of the environment (e.g., looking away from threats or being unable to look away from threats) or the selection of certain features of the environment (e.g., when scanning emotional faces). Memory processes encompasses (restricted) access to semantic content and episodic experiences reported in a deliberate manner. They also include recognition and the use of procedural or script knowledge assessed by implicit or behavioral measures.

Table 4.1. Structure and Functions of Internal Working Models

Functions	Control Level	
Information Processing	Implicit-Procedural	Evaluative-Declarative
Perception	Automated, intuitive: Allocation of attention Pattern recognition	Conscious awareness: Voluntary control of attention Explicit access to perceived content
Memory	Implicit recognition/ episodic procedural scripts	Explicit semantic or episodic memory
Interpretation and prediction	Automated, intuitive appraisal of self and others: associated evaluations or feelings	Conscious appraisal and expectations regarding self and others
Emotion Regulation	Implicit-Procedural	Evaluative-Declarative
Regulation of emotion and behavior	Automated procedural rules "What to do when feeling bad" (e.g., proximity seeking, avoidance)	Conscious knowledge about possible solutions when experiencing distress

Source: Adapted from Zimmermann (1999).

Interpretation or prediction of others' intentions or emotions based on perceptions or memories can be accurate or can be positively or negatively biased.

The emotion regulation component of IWMs controls attachment behavior and exploration. It is based on the parallel information processing of relevant features of the environment or elicited memories and their interpretation is comparable to antecedent and response-focused emotion regulation. Many attachment researchers have emphasized that insecure attachment patterns are characterized by attentional restrictions when interacting with the attachment figure in the service of avoiding additional rejection (Bretherton, 1991; Main et al., 1985).

IWMs differ in their subjective level of accessibility. On a declarative-evaluative level, individuals are able to report voluntarily what they perceive, remember, or appraise and are able to report possible or applied strategies of what they do in distressing situations. This level of functioning may be applied mainly in nondistressing situations. However, when experiencing negative emotions, the implicit-procedural level of working models controls mainly automated information processing and emotion regulation, which may be more selective and faster, and attachment experiences may come into play. Bowlby (1980) emphasized that these two levels of accessibility and voluntary control of IWMs may describe why attachment experiences explain emotional disturbances despite the fact that individuals cannot report or clarify why they behave certain ways in specific situations. Bowlby's concept of IWMs therefore is an early form of a dual process theory (Evans, 2008), which is of special interest given the developmental changes in middle childhood.

During middle childhood, executive functioning becomes more effective (Carlson, Zelazo, & Faja, 2013), offering more voluntary monitoring and control of attentional processes. Cognitive development enables children to combine several different representations into single abstractions (Fischer & Bidell, 2006), which results in more sophisticated explicit voluntary appraisal skills. Emotional understanding then allows children to understand that others' emotions can be caused by incorrect assumptions and to explain the causes of complex and mixed emotions (Pons, Harris, & de Rosnay, 2004). Thus, although not yet as complex as in adolescence and adulthood, IWMs during middle childhood already begin to include reflective functioning (Delius, Bovenschen, & Spangler, 2008). However, these abilities may have more effect on the evaluative-declarative level and less on the implicit-procedural level.

Expected Effects of Attachment on Information Processing. According to Dykas and Cassidy (2011), individuals with secure IWMs of attachment, based on attachment figures' emotional availability and sensitive caregiving, process social stimuli in an open, positively biased, full, and flexible manner. In contrast, individuals with insecure IWMs of attachment process social stimuli in two possible ways: (1) by excluding social information in case it elicits psychological pain or feeling hurt, or (2) by processing social information in a negatively biased manner. The first process suggests that individuals with insecure attachment organization protect themselves from the experience of social pain and hurt feelings by defensive exclusion (Bowlby, 1980; Cassidy & Kobak, 1988). As studies in preschool, adolescence, and adulthood suggest (Dykas, Woodhouse, Jones, & Cassidy, 2014; Kirsh & Cassidy, 1997; Maier, Bernier, Pekrun, Zimmermann, Strasser, & Grossmann, 2005), such defensive processes become obvious by restricted or biased memory (on the evaluative-declarative level) and by involuntary selective attention (on the implicit-procedural level). The second process suggests that individuals with insecure attachment organizations expect rejection and ascribe negative intentions to others. Again, evidence for this finding exists in preschool, adolescence, and adulthood (Mikulincer & Shaver, 2005; Suess, Grossmann, & Sroufe, 1992; Zimmermann, 1999).

Attachment Effects on Information Processing in Middle Childhood: Empirical Evidence

Here we review the empirical evidence for associations between attachment and information processing in middle childhood, focusing on

attention, memory, interpretation, and prediction of others' behavior and
intentions.

Attachment and Attentional Processes in Middle Childhood. The
first evidence that early attachment influences attentional processes in middle childhood came from the Berkeley Longitudinal Study (Main et al.,
1985) showing that 6-year-old children who had been classified as insecure-
avoidant in the Strange Situation Procedure (SSP) in infancy (on a procedural level) avoided family portraits by turning away. In addition, Dykas
and Cassidy (2011) reported from the same study that children classified as
disorganized were not able to turn their attention away from these pictures.
Ziv, Oppenheim, and Sagi-Schwartz (2004) did not replicate these findings
in their study. However, they inferred children's attention from their accuracy in reproducing scenarios of peer group and mother–child interactions
presented on videotapes, which is a confounding of attentional and memory processes, so that their results are not directly comparable to those of
Main and colleagues (1985).

Vandevivere, Braet, Bosmans, Mueller, and de Raedt (2014) studied attachment and biased attentional processing in childhood (8–12 years) with
an eye-tracking paradigm. They presented neutral and emotional facial expressions of mother and female strangers and assessed attachment style explicitly by self-report. Children with avoidant attachment styles had fewer
fixations on mother's face compared to the stranger's faces in the emotion
condition, whereas children with secure attachment styles showed more fixations on mother's neutral face than on unfamiliar neutral faces. In addition,
they had longer viewing times on mother's emotional faces compared to
unfamiliar faces, whereas children with avoidant attachment styles showed
shorter viewing time on mother's emotional faces compared to stranger's facial expressions. These results suggest that an avoidant attachment stance
toward mother that is explicitly reported and evaluated in a questionnaire
leads to attentional avoidance of mother's face compared to unfamiliar faces
when expressing emotions and to lower interest in mother's face when expressing no emotions. Focusing on IWMs of attachment, Bosmans, Braet,
Koster, and de Raedt (2009) assessed the associations of explicit attachment
measures and the breadth of attention around mother in children 9 to 12
years old. They presented pictures of mother or unfamiliar women in a dual
task paradigm and measured trust, alienation, and attachment styles explicitly by self-report. Attachment style was not significantly associated with
attentional breadth. However, the trust score, as an indicator of explicitly
evaluated attachment security, was significantly associated with an attentional focus on pictures of mother in the preattentive stage of information
processing (34 milliseconds [ms]). Thus, during fast early information processing, children with low trust in their mothers seem to be vigilant toward
them.

Similar effects are found in children with highly neglecting and abu-
sive caregiving experiences who developed reactive attachment disorders

NEW DIRECTIONS FOR CHILD AND ADOLESCENT DEVELOPMENT • DOI: 10.1002/cad

(RADs), a diagnosis clearly distinguished from usual attachment patterns by a failure to show selective attachment (O'Connor & Zeanah, 2003). Both the indiscriminate friendliness of the disinhibited type and the frozen watchfulness of the inhibited type may be signs of disorder-specific attentional processes. Zimmermann and Meier (2011) studied earlier and later stages of attention regulation in a sample of 10-year-olds with clinical diagnosis of RAD in a dot-probe paradigm with emotional faces, social interaction scenes, and neutral reaction time measures. The children with RAD showed longer reaction times during presentation of social and emotional pictures compared to neutral pictures. This finding suggests that children with attachment disorders have difficulties allocating attention away from social contexts. In addition, they showed attentional vigilance toward pictures of rejection at 100 ms and attentional avoidance at 500 ms presentation time. This finding suggests a primary attentional vigilance toward rejection, a well-known experience in these children, followed by an attentional avoidance as an applied emotion regulation strategy.

Thus, there is some evidence that early avoidant and disorganized attachment assessed on the procedural level is influencing attentional processes in middle childhood. In addition, findings about concurrent attachment assessed on the explicit-evaluative level support the hypothesis of an attachment-attention association in middle childhood. Attachment avoidance leads to an automated early vigilance toward mother's face, followed by attentional avoidance in case of stimuli that show emotional expressions. This pattern of attentional regulation of early vigilance toward family-related stimuli and later application of attentional avoidance as an emotion regulation strategy for insecure-avoidant attached children supports Bretherton's (1991) idea that these children are quite vigilant toward their close social environment, perhaps in order to be successful in their avoidant attachment strategy. Similar attentional processes may be functional in children with RADs. However, replications and additional studies including the insecure-resistant category would help to clarify the attentional mechanisms.

Attachment and Memory. There already is some evidence for effects of infant attachment on memory processes for social stimuli in early childhood (Belsky, Spitz, & Crnic, 1996; Kirsh & Cassidy, 1997), although there also are studies showing no longitudinal effects (Ziv et al., 2004). Dykas and Cassidy (2011) explained inconsistent findings by different research designs and memory tasks. Dujardin, Bosmans, Braet, and Goossens (2014) assessed trust in maternal support during middle childhood as an indicator of attachment security at an explicit-declarative level. They tested memory for adjectives describing the child's emotions in interaction with mother in a modification of the levels of processing task (LOP; Rudolph, Hammen, & Burge, 1995) in a sample of children aged 10 to 12. Results showed a negative mother-related memory bias for children with lower trust scores. Thus, children with a more insecure attachment representation of mother remembered more mother-related negative words. Lynch and Cicchetti (1998) also used a modification of the LOP task with traumatized children (maltreatment and community violence). Relationship quality to mother was assessed at the explicit-evaluative level by means of self-report. An optimal pattern of relatedness with high levels of positive emotions and low levels of need for more proximity served as an attachment indicator. Results showed that maltreated children with secure patterns of relatedness recalled a higher proportion of positive words that they had rated before as not describing their mothers compared to maltreated children with insecure relatedness. Surprisingly, children traumatized by experiencing community violence and an insecure pattern of relatedness also recalled more positive attributes that they said did not describe their mothers. Alexander, O'Hara, Bortfeld, Anderson, Newton, and Kraft (2010) assessed attachment security on an explicit-evaluative level and found that 7- to 12-year-olds with higher attachment security scores had better memory for negative attachment-related information (e.g., separation). Interestingly, attachment security did not influence memory for positive attachment-related information.

Taken together, although diverging, the findings show that for all these explicit measures of attachment or relationship quality, felt security to mother influences memory processes. However, the studies did not differentiate between the insecure-avoidant and the insecure-resistant attachment pattern. It may well be the case that the positive association between attachment insecurity and the negative mother-related memory bias might be more typical for an underlying insecure-resistant attachment organization, where negative emotions are easy elicited when thinking about the relationship to mother. In contrast, the poor memory for negative attachment-related information (e.g., separation) might be an indicator of an underlying avoidant pattern, where defensive exclusion (i.e., not remembering hurtful events) would be a marker of the insecure-avoidant emotion regulation strategy of minimizing the engagement with attachment-relevant information. This finding might be highly relevant for autobiographical events (Bosmans, Dujardin, Raes, & Braet, 2013). We see three lacunas: (1) a lack of research using attachment assessments on the implicit-procedural level, (2) a lack of differentiation of the insecure attachment patterns, and (3) a need for more research on memory of autobiographical or family interactions.

Attachment and the Interpretation of Social Situations. Most research on attachment and information processing in middle childhood is on the interpretation of social or emotional stimuli. The studies capture different aspects of interpretation processes: attributions of others' intentions, theory of mind ability, emotion understanding, and recognition of other's emotions.

Attachment and Attributional Bias. Cassidy (1988) showed that insecure attachment patterns at age 6 (assessed at an implicit-procedural level;

reunion paradigm) were significantly associated with the appraisal of lower peer acceptance. Cassidy, Kirsh, Scolton, and Parke (1996) reported a negative social attributional bias in insecurely attached first graders when interpreting ambiguous social situations. Insecurely attached children (Main & Cassidy, 1988; reunion classification system) showed a negative bias in the perception of their peers' feelings and underlying intentions and motives. Zaccagnino, Cussino, Callerame, Actis Perinetti, Veglia, and Green (2013) reported that children 4 to 7 years old classified as disorganized in a story stem task showed a hostile attributional bias in a social cognition task. Ziv and colleagues (2004) assessed children's interpretation accuracy of peer and mother–child interactions presented on videotapes in comparison to expert ratings. They found no attachment differences (secure versus resistant and disorganized) for the peer rejection stories but significant differences for the mother–child interaction stories. Children classified as securely attached in infancy interpreted the mother's responses to stressful situations on the videotapes as more positive, sensitive, and understanding compared to insecurely attached children (without avoidant classification). Securely attached children seem to apply their IWMs based on their own supportive attachment history when interpreting other unknown mother–child dyads. Granot and Mayseless (2012) reported similar results for 10-year-olds. In a study using story stem (an implicit-procedural interpretation of the play), securely attached children showed more prosocial information processing than children classified as insecure avoidant. In contrast, disorganized attachment was positively associated with antisocial processing. Furthermore, Dwyer, Fredstrom, Rubin, Booth-LaForce, Rose-Krasnor, and Burgess (2010) showed an association between maladaptive social information processing (attribution of internal and external blame) and lower levels of attachment security to father (using Kerns's Security Scale) in a sample of 11-year-old children. Brumariu, Kerns, and Seibert (2012) tested associations of attachment and interpretation biases of emotional events in 10- to 12-year-olds. Using an adapted story stem to assess representations of mother–child attachment, they found no associations between organized attachment patterns and biased appraisal of emotionally charged events. However, children classified as disorganized revealed a negative interpretation bias with increased catastrophizing during the scenarios (a sign of disorganization in some classification systems). Thus, the different attachment measure might have influenced the divergent evidence. Evidence for insecure-resistant attachment is clearly missing.

Attachment and Theory of Mind. Theory of mind (ToM) is the individual's knowledge and understanding that others' mental states are independent from one's own state and that mental states influence behavior (Wellman, 1990). In preschool, securely attached children showed a better ToM performance compared to insecurely attached children (De Rosnay & Harris, 2002; McElwain & Volling, 2004). Humfress, O'Connor, Slaughter, Target, and Fonagy (2002) reported for 12-year-old children that lower scores in attachment coherency (in the Child Attachment Interview [CAI]; Target, Fonagy, & Shmueli-Goetz, 2003) were associated with a less differentiated understanding of the influence of mental states on the behavior of main characters in short stories. Despite the ample evidence for an attachment effect on ToM performance, it remains yet unclear whether the insecure attachment patterns differ in their ability to understand ToM.

Attachment, Emotion Understanding, and Emotion Recognition. There is evidence for attachment effects on emotion understanding and recognition in middle childhood that are similar to those in studies in preschool (Laible & Thompson, 1998). Steele, Steele, Croft, and Fonagy (1999) reported that children classified as securely attached in infancy (in the SSP) performed better at age 6 in identifying and justifying others' emotions in social and emotional dilemma situations. In a sample of 10-year-olds, Zimmermann (2006) found that insecure attachment behavior and representation (assessed by the Late Childhood Attachment Interview [LCAI]; Zimmermann & Scheuerer-Englisch, 2000) were significantly associated with more errors in emotion recognition of adult expressions presented in a morph task for the emotions of anger and sadness but not for joy and fear. This deficit in correct emotion recognition partly explained why insecurely attached children are more aggressive.

Taken together, secure attachment in middle childhood is associated with an expectation of others' positive intentions and prosocial behaviors and with not easily feeling alienated. In addition, securely attached children more easily understand others' perspectives and are more accurate in recognizing others' emotions. Insecurely attached children more often expect rejection from others or ascribe negative intentions to others. However, the number of studies in this area is still relatively small. There is more research on the interpretation of peer interactions and very little on interactions with family members in middle childhood. In addition, studies do not always differentiate between all insecure attachment groups. Evidence regarding an attributional bias in insecure-resistant attachment in middle childhood is sparse. A hostile attributional bias seems to be more common in children with disorganized attachment classifications. This might explain their higher rates of aggressive or externalizing behavior (Moss & Lecompte, Article 5, this issue).

New Directions in Middle Childhood Attachment Research

The published empirical work on attachment and information processing in middle childhood is relatively small, compared to other age groups. This is especially true for studies on attention modulation, memory processes, and emotion recognition, whereas studies on attributional bias or perspective taking are quite common.

The small number of studies may result from the fact that a variety of assessment measures for that age period, ranging from self-reports to interview approaches (Bosmans & Kerns, Article 1, this issue), may tap into different areas of attachment and IWMs, but no defined gold standard exists yet. The existing studies are not yet comparable, as they use many different assessment approaches for attachment that do not always differentiate between the insecure attachment patterns. As defensive processes are also present when reporting about attachment experiences, it seems quite plausible that self-reported attachment styles and interview-based attachment patterns are only partly concordant, as is the case in adult attachment measures. This might lead to different results.

Therefore, one new direction in research on attachment and information processing in middle childhood is the parallel use of different attachment measures that tap into the implicit-procedural and the declarative-evaluative level of IWMs. Thus, a combination of self-report with interview approaches in the same study or the use of implicit-procedural assessments like the prompt-word outline method (Waters & Waters, 2006) or the Implicit Association Test (IAT) for attachment (Zimmermann & Maier, 2001) will offer empirical evidence regarding what level of attachment assessment predicts what kind of information processing.

A second new direction would be the expansion of research in information processing in the area of personal or autobiographical content. There is a clear need for additional research on autobiographical memory and family interactions comparable to studies for older age groups and in the processing of information about the self.

Another new direction should be an increased interest in differentiating the information processing of children with insecure-avoidant, insecure-resistant, and disorganized attachment. Insecure attachment in middle childhood is associated with emotional unavailability of the caregivers, but the attachment patterns represent different strategies how to deal with the felt insecurity. There is a clear lacuna in research on information processing in children with an insecure-resistant attachment pattern and with disorganized attachment. Nearly no research has tested whether a hyperactivating strategy characterizes insecure-resistant attachment, as assumed for infancy and adulthood (Cassidy, 1995). It may well be that these children also develop other strategies or that avoiding or passive strategies in information processing are learned during middle childhood.

Finally, there is too little research applying a two-factor model approach of information processing in middle childhood that makes use of different levels of accessibility of information processing. Starting with Bowlby (1980), many attachment theorists have emphasized the difference between conscious, deliberate information processing and implicit, automated processing. However, only some of the studies in middle childhood apply this idea. Studying implicit attentional processes, social cognition, or memory will help to elucidate the differences between the insecure attachment groups in middle childhood. There are some hints that the insecure-avoidant attachment pattern might result in a regulation of attention that first shows fast vigilance to attachment-related stimuli followed by an avoidance of these stimuli. Attentional avoidance is then a slower second step in the modulation of attention to downregulate emotional arousal that potentially elicit hurt feelings, for example, in the case of rejection. Such research could help corroborate whether concurrent attachment disorganization in middle childhood is indeed associated with an inability to allocate attention away from distressing stimuli (Dykas & Cassidy, 2011), as a breakdown of an organized or regulating attachment strategy.

References

Ainsworth, M. D. S., Blehar, M., Waters, E., & Wall, S. (1978). *Patterns of attachment. A psychological study of the strange situation*. Hillsdale, NJ: Erlbaum.

Alexander, K. W., O'Hara, K. D., Bortfeld, H. V., Anderson, S. J., Newton, E. K., & Kraft, R. H. (2010). Memory for emotional experiences in the context of attachment and social interaction style. *Cognitive Development, 25*, 325–338.

Belsky, J., & de Haan, M. (2011). Annual Research Review: Parenting and children's brain development: The end of the beginning. *Journal of Child Psychology and Psychiatry, 52*, 409–428.

Belsky, J., Spitz, B., & Crnic, K. (1996). Infant attachment security and affective-cognitive information processing at age 3. *Psychological Science, 7*, 111–114.

Bosmans, G., Braet, C., Koster, E., & de Raedt, R. (2009). Attachment security and attentional breadth toward attachment figure in middle childhood. *Journal of Clinical Child & Adolescent Psychology, 38*, 872–882.

Bosmans, G., Dujardin, A., Raes, F., & Braet, C. (2013). The specificity of autobiographical attachment memories in early adolescence: The role of mother-child communication and attachment-related beliefs. *Journal of Early Adolescence, 33*, 710–731.

Bowlby, J. (1973). *Attachment and loss: Vol. 2. Separation: Anxiety and anger*. New York, NY: Basic Books.

Bowlby, J. (1980). *Attachment and loss. Vol. 3. Loss, sadness, and depression*. New York, NY: Basic Books.

Bowlby, J. (1988). *A secure base*. New York, NY: Basic Books.

Bretherton, I. (1991). Pouring new wine into old bottles: The social self as internal working model. In M. Gunnar & L. A. Sroufe (Eds.), *Minnesota Symposia on Child Psychology: Vol. 23. Self processes in development* (pp. 1–41). Hillsdale, NJ: Erlbaum.

Bretherton, I., & Munholland, K. (2008). Internal working models in attachment relationships: Elaborating a central construct in attachment theory. In J. Cassidy & P. Shaver (Eds.), *Handbook of attachment: Theory, research, and clinical applications* (2nd ed., pp. 102–130). New York, NY: Guilford Press.

Brumariu, L., Kerns, K., & Seibert, A. (2012). Mother-child attachment, emotion regulation, and anxiety symptoms in middle childhood. *Personal Relationships, 19*, 569–585.

Carlson, S. M., Zelazo, P. D., & Faja, S. (2013). Executive function. In P. D. Zelazo (Ed.), *Oxford handbook of developmental psychology, Vol. 1: Body and mind* (pp. 706–743). New York, NY: Oxford University Press.

Cassidy, J. (1988). Child-mother attachment and the self in six-year-olds. *Child Development, 59*, 121–134.

Cassidy, J. (1995). Emotion regulation. Influences of attachment relationships. *Monographs of the Society for Research in Child Development, 59*, 228–249.

Cassidy, J., Kirsh, S., Scolton, K., & Parke, R. (1996). Attachment and representations of peer relationships. *Developmental Psychology, 32*, 892–904.

Cassidy, J., & Kobak, R. (1988). Avoidance and its relation to other defensive processes. In J. Belsky & T. Nezworski (Eds.), *Clinical implications of attachment* (pp. 300–323). Hillsdale, NJ: Erlbaum.

Colvert, E., Rutter, M., Kreppner, J., Beckett, C., Castle, J., Groothues, C., . . . Sonuga-Barke, E. J. (2008). Do theory of mind and executive function deficits underlie the adverse outcomes associated with profound early deprivation? Findings from the English and Romanian Adoptees Study. *Journal of Abnormal Child Psychology*, 7, 1057–1068.

Crick, N. R., & Dodge, K. A. (1994). A review and reformulation of social information-processing mechanisms in children's social adjustment. *Psychological Bulletin*, 115, 74–101.

Delius, A., Bovenschen, I., & Spangler, G. (2008). The inner working model as a "theory of attachment": Development during the preschool years. *Attachment & Human Development*, 10, 395–414.

De Rosnay, M., & Harris, P. (2002). Individual differences in children's understanding of emotion: The roles of attachment and language. *Attachment & Human Development*, 4, 39–54.

Dujardin, A., Bosmans, G., Braet, C., & Goossens, L. (2014). Attachment-related expectations and mother-referent memory bias in middle childhood. *Scandinavian Journal of Psychology*, 55, 296–302.

Dwyer, K. M., Fredstrom, B., Rubin, K., Booth-LaForce, C., Rose-Kransor, L., & Burgess, K. (2010). Attachment, social information processing, and friendship quality of early adolescent girls and boys. *Journal of Social and Personal Relationships*, 27, 91–116.

Dykas, M. J., & Cassidy, J. (2011). Attachment and the processing of social information across the life span: Theory and evidence. *Psychological Bulletin*, 137, 19–46.

Dykas, M. J., Woodhouse, S. S., Jones, J. D., & Cassidy, J. (2014). Attachment-related biases in adolescents' memory. *Child Development*, 85, 2185–2201.

Eisenberg, N., Cumberland, A., & Spinrad, T. L. (1998). Parental socialization of emotion. *Psychological Inquiry*, 9, 241–273.

Evans, J. S. B. (2008). Dual-processing accounts of reasoning, judgment, and social cognition. *Annual Review of Psychology*, 59, 255–278.

Fischer, K. W., & Bidell, T. R. (2006). Dynamic development of action, thought, and emotion. In W. Damon & R. M. Lerner (Eds.), *Handbook of child psychology* (Vol. 1, pp. 313–399). Chichester, UK: Wiley.

Granot, D., & Mayseless, O. (2012). Representations of mother-child attachment relationships and social-information processing of peer relationships in early adolescence. *Journal of Early Adolescence*, 32, 537–564.

Grossmann, K. E., Grossmann, K., Kindler, H., & Zimmermann, P. (2008). A wider view of attachment and exploration: The influence of mothers and fathers on the development of psychological security from infancy to young adulthood. In J. Cassidy & P. Shaver (Eds.), *Handbook of attachment theory, research, and clinical applications* (pp. 857–879). New York, NY: Guilford Press.

Humfress, H., O'Connor, T., Slaughter, J., Target, M., & Fonagy, P. (2002). General and relationship-specific models of social cognition: Explaining the overlap and discrepancies. *Journal of Child Psychology & Psychiatry*, 43, 873–883.

Kirsh, S., & Cassidy, J. (1997). Preschoolers' attention and memory for attachment-relevant information. *Child Development*, 68, 1143–1153.

Laible, D. J., & Thompson, R. A. (1998). Attachment and emotional understanding in preschool children. *Developmental Psychology*, 34, 1038–1045.

Lemerise, E. A., & Arsenio, W. F. (2000). An integrated model of emotion processes and cognition in social information processing. *Child Development*, 71, 107–118.

Lynch, M., & Cicchetti, D. (1998). An ecological-transactional analysis of children and contexts: The longitudinal interplay among child maltreatment, community violence, and children's symptomatology. *Development and Psychopathology*, 10, 235–257.

Maier, M. A., Bernier, A., Pekrun, R., Zimmermann, P., Strasser, K., & Grossmann, K. E. (2005). Attachment state of mind and perceptual processing of emotional stimuli. *Attachment & Human Development, 7*, 67–81.

Main, M., & Cassidy, J. (1988). Categories of response to reunion with the parent at age 6: Predictable from infant attachment classifications and stable over 1-month period. *Developmental Psychology, 24*, 415–426.

Main, M., Kaplan, N., & Cassidy, J. (1985). Security in infancy, childhood, and adulthood: A move to the level of representation. *Monographs of the Society for Research in Child Development, 50*(1–2), 66–104.

Massaro, D. W., & Cowan, N. (1993). Information processing models: Microscopes of the mind. *Annual Review of Psychology, 44*, 383–425.

McElwain, N., & Volling, B. (2004). Attachment security and parental sensitivity during infancy: Associations with friendship quality and false-belief understanding at age 4. *Journal of Social and Personal Relationships, 21*, 639–667.

Meyer, S., Raikes, H., Virmani, E., Waters, S., & Thompson, R. A. (2014). Parent emotion representations and the socialization of emotion regulation in the family. *International Journal of Behavioral Development, 38*, 164–173.

Mikulincer, M., & Shaver, P. R. (2005). Attachment theory and emotions in close relationships: Exploring the attachment-related dynamics of emotional reactions to relational events. *Personal Relationships, 12*, 149–168.

O'Connor, T. G., & Zeanah, C. H. (2003). Attachment disorders: Assessment strategies and treatment approaches. *Attachment & Human Development, 5*, 223–244.

Pollak, S., & Sinha, P. (2004). Effects of early experience on children's recognition of facial displays of emotion. *Developmental Psychology, 38*, 784–791.

Pons, F., Harris, P., & de Rosnay, M. (2004). Emotion comprehension between 3 and 11 years: Developmental periods and hierarchical organization. *European Journal of Developmental Psychology, 1*, 127–152.

Rudolph, K., Hammen, C., & Burge, D. (1995). Cognitive representations of self, family, and peers in school-aged-children—links with social competence and sociometric status. *Child Development, 66*, 1385–1402.

Spangler, G., & Grossmann, K. (1993). Biobehavioral organization in securely and insecurely attached infants. *Child Development, 64*, 1439–1450.

Spangler, G., & Zimmermann, P. (2014). Emotional and adrenocortical regulation in early adolescence: Prediction by security and disorganization in infancy. *International Journal of Behavioral Development, 38*, 142–154.

Steele, H., Steele, M., Croft, C., & Fonagy, P. (1999). Infant-mother attachment at one year predicts children's understanding of mixed emotions at six years. *Social Development, 8*, 161–178.

Suess, G., Grossmann, K., & Sroufe, L. A. (1992). Effects of infant attachment to mother and father on quality of adaptation in preschool: From dyadic to individual organization of self. *International Journal of Behavioral Development, 15*, 43–65.

Target, M., Fonagy, P., & Shmueli-Goetz, Y. (2003). Attachment representations in school-age children: The development of the Child Attachment Interview (CAI). *Journal of Child Psychotherapy, 29*, 171–186.

Vandevivere, E., Braet, C., Bosmans, G., Mueller, S., & de Raedt, R. (2014). Attachment and children's biased attentional processing: Evidence for the exclusion of attachment-related information. *Plos One, 9*, e103476.

Waters, E., & Cummings, E. (2000). A secure base from which to explore close relationships. *Child Development, 71*, 164–172.

Waters, H., & Waters, E. (2006). The attachment working models concept: Among other things, we build script-like representations of secure base experiences. *Attachment & Human Development, 8*, 185–197.

Wellman, H. (1990). *The child's theory of mind.* Cambridge, MA: MIT Press.

Zaccagnino, M., Cussino, M., Callerame, C., Actis Perinetti, B., Veglia, F., & Green, J. (2013). Attachment and social understanding in young school-age children: An investigation using the Manchester Child Attachment Story Task. *Minerva Psichiatrica, 54*, 59–69.

Zimmermann, P. (1999). Structure and functions of internal working models of attachment and their role for emotion regulation. *Attachment & Human Development, 1*, 291–307.

Zimmermann, P. (2006, August). *Attachment, emotion recognition, and aggression.* Paper presented at the 13th European Conference on Developmental Psychology, Jena, Germany.

Zimmermann, P., & Maier, M. (2001, August). *Implicit and explicit attachment representations.* Paper presented at the 11th European Conference on Developmental Psychology, Milan, Italy.

Zimmermann, P., Maier, M., Winter, M., & Grossmann, K. (2001). Attachment and emotion regulation of adolescents during joint problem-solving with a friend. *International Journal of Behavioral Development, 25*, 331–342.

Zimmermann, P., & Meier, S. (2011, April). *Comparing children with reactive attachment disorder and ADHD: Differences in personality and information processing.* Paper presented at the biennial meeting of the Society for Research on Child Development, Montreal, Canada.

Zimmermann, P., & Scheuerer-Englisch, H. (2000). *Late Childhood Attachment Interview and coding manual.* Regensburg, Germany: University of Regensburg.

Ziv, Y., Oppenheim, D., & Sagi-Schwartz, A. (2004). Social information processing in middle childhood: Relations to infant-mother attachment. *Attachment & Human Development, 6*, 327–348.

PETER ZIMMERMANN, PhD, *is a professor of developmental psychology at the University of Wuppertal.*

ALEXANDRA IWANSKI, PhD, *is a lecturer of developmental psychology at the University of Wuppertal.*

Moss, E., & Lecompte, V. (2015). Attachment and socioemotional problems in middle childhood. In G. Bosmans & K. A. Kerns (Eds.), *Attachment in middle childhood: Theoretical
advances and new directions in an emerging field. New Directions for Child and Adolescent
Development, 148,* 63–76.

Attachment and Socioemotional Problems in Middle Childhood

Ellen Moss, Vanessa Lecompte

Abstract

*In this article, we will evaluate the evidence concerning links between attach-
ment and behavior problems in the middle childhood period. We will first provide a general introduction to the question of attachment and maladaptation in
the middle childhood period, and then examine the recent empirical evidence
with respect to both externalizing and internalizing profiles. We will conclude
with a discussion of new directions in research on this issue including the search
for possible mediators and moderators of attachment/behavior problem associations. © 2015 Wiley Periodicals, Inc.*

T he attachment relationship was conceptualized by John Bowlby (1969) as serving an adaptive function relevant to the life span rather than to restricted periods of development only. In middle childhood, the importance of the attachment relationship remains high, and children continue to need and rely on attachment figures across childhood and adolescence (Bowlby, 1989). In this article, we examine links between measures of attachment and socioemotional problems in middle childhood. Although both representational and behavioral measures of attachment are important in examining this question, we limit our focus here to those studies using behavioral measures assessed in parent–child interactive contexts, primarily separation–reunion. Given the conceptual differences between representational and behavioral measures and the paucity of studies assessing their associations, lumping together results of outcome studies using these different measures may add confusion rather than clarity to the literature. In addition, studies using representational measures, which report similar effects of attachment on socioemotional outcomes, are covered in other articles in this issue (Bosmans & Kerns, Article 1; Brumariu, Article 3; Zimmermann & Iwanski, Article 4).

There is considerable conceptual similarity among the behavioral measures of attachment based on separation–reunion behavior (Ainsworth, Blehar, Waters, & Wall, 1978; Cassidy, Marvin, & MacArthur Attachment Working Group, 1992; Main & Cassidy, 1988) used in infancy, preschool, and the early–middle childhood period. All evaluate the extent to which children are able to use the caregiver as source of comfort and a secure base for exploration and use a four-classification coding scheme—A: avoidant, B: secure, C: ambivalent, D: disorganized/controlling—based on observations of the child's physical proximity to mother, affective expression, and verbal exchanges. Numerous studies have established the reliability of separation–reunion measures from age 1 to 7 (Ainsworth et al., 1978; Moss, Bureau, St.-Laurent, Cyr, & Mongeau, 2004), as well as some degree of stability of attachment for this age period (Moss, Cyr, Bureau, Tarabulsy, & Dubois-Comtois, 2005).

Attachment and the Development of Externalizing Behavior Problems

The recent publication of an important meta-analysis (Fearon, Bakermans-Kranenburg, van Ijzendoorn, Lapsley, & Roisman, 2010) provides an overview of the empirical links between attachment and externalizing problems. Fearon and colleagues examined the predictive significance of attachment for later externalizing problems using data from 69 samples ($N = 5,947$). Externalizing behavior was defined as aggression, oppositional problems, conduct problems, or hostility as assessed by observations, clinical interview, or teacher or parent report. Analyses included only studies using observational measures of mother–child attachment (e.g., the Strange Situation Procedure [SSP], Ainsworth et al., 1978; Preschool Attachment Classification System [PACS], Cassidy et al., 1992; Main and Cassidy System, Main & Cassidy, 1988). Results showed a significant association between insecure attachment and externalizing problems with a modest but robust effect size ($d = 0.31$, 95% confidence interval [CI] $0.06\sim0.25$). The relevance of this study for the middle childhood period is underscored by the fact that samples of children aged 12 years or younger were included, and the age of the child at the time of the outcome assessment was not significantly associated with the magnitude of study effect sizes. In addition, the authors reported that effect sizes increased significantly over time, suggesting that associations are stronger in middle childhood than in early childhood. This finding is consistent with the results of studies that have examined this question using middle childhood samples (e.g., Dubois-Comtois, Moss, Cyr, & Pascuzzo, 2013; Moss, Cyr, & Dubois-Comtois, 2004; Solomon, George, & DeJong, 1995).

Given the very different behavioral profiles that characterize children with insecure attachment patterns, it is important to evaluate the risk associated with each insecure attachment group. An important distinction is between the insecure-organized (avoidant and ambivalent) and disorganized groups. Children with organized-insecure attachment patterns are generally considered to be situated midway on the risk continuum between the secure and disorganized groups. This is not surprising, given that much greater behavioral dysregulation is associated with disorganization, as are higher levels of family risk and maternal psychosocial distress (Moss, Cyr, & Dubois-Comtois, 2004). However, there has been controversy concerning the predictive significance of all insecure patterns—that is, disorganization, avoidance, and ambivalence—for externalizing psychopathology in general (Belsky & Fearon, 2002; NICHD Early Child Care Research Network, 2006) and with respect to the middle childhood period in particular (Kerns, 2008).

In examining associations for insecure groups, Fearon et al. (2010) reported that the meta-analytic association between disorganized attachment and externalizing problems was as strong as that found for insecure attachment ($d = 0.34$, 95% CI $0.18\sim0.50$), echoing findings from previous studies examining this association in middle childhood (e.g., Dubois-Comtois et al., 2013; O'Connor, Bureau, McCartney, & Lyons-Ruth, 2011). These robust associations between both insecurity and disorganization and externalizing problems strongly support the role of attachment as a prominent risk factor for externalizing problems.

With respect to the role of insecure-organized attachment patterns in predicting externalizing problems, Fearon et al. (2010) found that avoidant and resistant children displayed a slightly higher level (respective effect sizes $d = 0.12$, 95% CI $0.03\sim0.21$; $d = 0.11$, 95% CI $-0.04\sim0.26$) than did secure children. This finding is generally consistent with the current middle childhood literature, which has shown inconsistent attachment/externalizing problem associations for these groups. Several longitudinal studies using four-way classification schemes have found that avoidant children, assessed using early childhood separation–reunion measures, had higher externalizing problems in middle childhood than did secure children (Fearon & Belsky, 2011; Munson, McMahon, & Spieker, 2001), but others have found no association (Dubois-Comtois et al., 2013; Moss, Cyr, & Dubois-Comtois, 2004). Similarly, ambivalent children have been found, in several studies, to show greater externalizing problems than secure children (Dubois-Comtois et al., 2013; Moss et al., 2006), but not in others (Fearon & Belsky, 2011; Lyons-Ruth, Easterbrooks, & Cibelli, 1997).

These discrepancies may be explained by the fact that studies which have used preschool and early middle childhood measures of attachment are more likely to report positive associations between ambivalence and externalizing problems than those using infant measures, whereas the opposite is true for avoidance (Dubois-Comtois et al., 2013; NICHD Early Child Care Research Network, 2004). As suggested by Vershueren and Marcoen (1999), the maintenance of exaggerated dependency on parental figures in early childhood, when parent–child coregulation of affective states is critical, may not be maladaptive unless it is maintained through middle childhood and beyond. Similarly, avoidance may be particularly maladaptive in infancy but less so through middle childhood, when greater independence may even facilitate integration in extrafamilial settings (Moss, Pascuzzo, & Simard, 2012). Of course, in adolescence, with its increasing demands for intimacy in peer relationships, the strength of associations between avoidance and ambivalence and externalizing problems may shift. A second important factor to consider is that mother and child reports regarding the ambivalent group may exaggerate negative behavioral profiles, whereas those for the avoidant group may idealize and minimize the expression of negativity. Methodologically, it is therefore important to consider multiple reporters when evaluating outcomes.

Attachment and the Development of Internalizing Behavior Problems

Two meta-analyses (Groh, Roisman, van Ijzendoorn, Bakermans-Kranenburg, & Fearon, 2012; Madigan, Atkinson, Laurin, & Benoit, 2012) and one narrative review (Brumariu & Kerns, 2010) have recently investigated the association between attachment and internalizing problems. The Groh et al. (2012) study analyzed data from 42 samples ($N =$ 4,614) of children aged 24 to 168 months, using criteria for inclusion similar to that in Fearon et al. (2010). Madigan et al. (2012) examined 60 studies ($N = 5,236$) including children aged 12 to 96 months. The definition of internalizing symptoms in both studies included depression, anxiety, social isolation, withdrawal, and somatic complaints. The relevance of both studies for the middle childhood period is underscored by reporting of outcomes for children 12 years and younger. More precisely, 21 studies included outcomes for children aged between 6 and 12 years in the Groh meta-analysis, and 14 studies included outcomes for children of those ages in the Madigan meta-analysis. Brumariu and Kerns (2010) conducted an important comprehensive narrative review of 55 studies including children 18 years and younger. Major differences between this review and the meta-analyses was the inclusion of adolescents and a much broader array of attachment measures, behavioral as well as representational.

In line with findings for externalizing problems, a significant association was found between insecure attachment and internalizing problems in both the Groh and Madigan meta-analyses. However, effect sizes were weaker than that found for externalizing symptomatology (respectively $d = 0.15$, 95% CI 0.06~0.25 Groh; $d = 0.19$, 95% CI 0.09~0.30 Madigan). Brumariu and Kerns (2010) arrived at a similar conclusion in their narrative review, further specifying that associations may be strongest for specific symptomatology—that is, anxiety and depression—in the preadolescent/ adolescent period, and when representational measures are used (inclusion criteria not applicable to the meta-analyses).

In contrast with results for externalizing problems (Fearon et al., 2010), meta-analytic associations between disorganization and overall internalizing problems were not significant. However, in line with Brumariu and Kerns (2010), we feel that it would be premature to conclude that disorganization is not linked to internalizing symptoms in middle childhood. For one thing, internalizing symptoms become increasingly demarcated as children advance in age. Thus, effect sizes based on combined early and later childhood outcomes may mask a significant association for the middle childhood period. This finding is supported by studies showing that depression, anxieties, and fears related to performance, abilities, and self-worth are associated with disorganization in middle childhood and adolescence (e.g., Brumariu, Kerns, & Seibert, 2012; Lecompte, Moss, Cyr, & Pascuzzo, 2014; Moss et al., 2006). In addition, the Madigan and Groh meta-analyses selected associations based on maternal reports, in cases of multiple reporters. Given children's increasing reluctance to share internalizing symptoms with adults, despite the increase in such symptoms during middle childhood (Edelbrock, Costello, Dulcan, Kalas, & Conover, 1985), self-report measures may be a more important source of information than parental reports on internalizing symptomatology for that period.

It is particularly interesting that, in both meta-analyses, avoidant children were found to have heightened risk for internalizing problems (respective effect sizes $d = 0.17$, 95% CI 0.03~0.31 Groh; $d = 0.29$, 95% CI

0.12~0.45 Madigan). This is consistent with the behavioral observations of avoidant children during stress-inducing contexts, which show minimization of negative affective expression and withdrawal in the presence of the caregiver (Moss et al., 2012). Studies using observational measures of attachment with middle childhood outcomes have also shown this pattern (Bureau & Moss, 2010; NICHD Early Child Care Research Network, 2006). Brumariu and Kerns (2010) did not conclude that avoidance heightened risk for internalizing problems. However, it should be noted that they included many studies which relied on self-reports of both attachment and problem outcomes. Avoidant children tend to idealize relationships with attachment figures and may minimize reporting of outcomes involving negative affective states (Moss et al., 2006).

Insecure ambivalence was not significantly associated with internalizing symptoms in either meta-analysis. This finding is consistent with the majority of studies that have used behavioral measures of attachment and assessed middle childhood outcomes (Manassis, 2011). It is also in line with observations of ambivalent children in preschool and middle childhood separation–reunion contexts that reveal heightened negative affective expression and conflictual modes of interaction, which are inconsistent with internalizing symptoms (Moss et al., 2012). In their narrative review, Brumariu and Kerns (2010) reported that studies using older samples and self-report outcome measures were more likely to reveal significant associations between insecure ambivalence and depression and anxiety. This is consistent with a few middle childhood studies that note similar associations with specific internalizing symptoms (Bar-Haim, Dan, Eshel, & Sagi-Schwartz, 2007; Warren, Huston, Egeland, & Sroufe, 1997). It is possible that the difficulties in parent–child emotion regulation that characterize the ambivalent pattern in the preschool/early school-age period may lead to the emergence of specific forms of internalizing symptomatology in preadolescence/adolescence. This may be more likely to occur if dyadic dysregulation is maintained or if the attachment figure has similar socioemotional problems.

Consideration of results from all three of these comprehensive studies shows the urgent need for further empirical research evaluating the links between different middle childhood measures of attachment and their relative predictive significance for psychopathology. The Brumariu and Kerns (2010) review is notable for differentiating between subtypes of internalizing problems (e.g., depression and anxiety) in assessing associations with different forms of insecurity. In fact, this suggestion has been empirically supported by recent middle childhood/preadolescent studies (Dubois-Comtois et al., 2013; Lecompte et al., 2014). In addition, results from meta-analyses and other studies that have considered the disorganized classification as a whole in evaluating associations with risk may not adequately reflect the situation for children showing different disorganized/controlling subtype patterns. This issue is discussed in the next section.

Associations Between Disorganized/Controlling Subtypes and Maladaptation

Between preschool and early school age, approximately two thirds of children earlier classified as disorganized assume a role-reversed relationship with their caregiver of a controlling–punitive or controlling–caregiving nature (Moss, Cyr, & Dubois-Comtois, 2004). The controlling–caregiving attachment strategy is characterized by a child's focus on helpfully guiding, orienting, or cheering up the parent. The controlling–punitive strategy involves the child's manifestation of hostile, directive behavior with the caregiver that may include verbal threats or harsh commands. Approximately one third of children earlier classified as disorganized do not show role reversal but continue to display the contradictory behavior patterns described earlier (Moss, Bureau, St.-Laurent, & Tarabulsy, 2011).

Currently, only seven studies have assessed behavior problems associated with the different disorganized subgroups in the preschool/middle childhood period (Bureau, Easterbrooks, & Lyons-Ruth, 2009; Dubois-Comtois et al., 2013; Lecompte & Moss, 2014; Moss, Cyr, & Dubois-Comtois, 2004; O'Connor et al., 2011; O'Connor & Spagnola, 2009; Teti, 1999). The most consistent finding to date is that children showing the controlling–punitive pattern are at greatest risk for elevated levels of externalizing problems during the late preschool/middle childhood period (e.g., Bureau et al., 2009; Dubois-Comtois et al., 2013; Lecompte & Moss, 2014; Moss, Cyr, & Dubois-Comtois, 2004). Several of these studies also show a comorbid profile with internalizing problems (e.g., Bureau et al., 2009; O'Connor et al., 2011). This is not surprising, given the hostile, aggressive child–parent interactive pattern that characterizes the controlling–punitive group and related difficulties with authority figures in school settings (Moss et al., 2012).

As for controlling–caregiving children, in two studies they were reported to present higher levels of internalizing problems, anxiety, and suicidal ideation (Dubois-Comtois et al., 2013; Moss, Cyr, & Dubois-Comtois, 2004) but were similar to their secure peers in two others (Bureau et al., 2009; O'Connor et al., 2011). Therefore, it is possible that other factors may moderate the trajectory for this group. Unlike the controlling–punitive pattern, which engenders aversive reactions in both home and school settings, controlling–caregiving children may be well liked by other adults. This opens the possibility that other attachment figures may play a compensatory role for some caregiving children and mitigate the risk trajectory.

Concerning behaviorally disorganized children, Bureau et al. (2009) and O'Connor and Spagnola (2009) found higher levels of internalizing and externalizing problems for this group in comparison to secure children; Moss, Cyr, and Dubois-Comtois (2004) and Dubois-Comtois et al. (2013) found only marginally greater levels of externalizing problems. In terms of behavior, this group is the most diverse with children showing the different atypical disorganized behaviors identified by Main and Solomon (1990). It is possible that some of these behaviors, such as freezing or crying while facing away from the caregiver, are more likely to be linked with internalizing symptoms, whereas others, such as striking the caregiver in the face, are linked to externalizing symptoms. At present, the number of behaviorally disorganized children in study samples does not allow for further subdivision. Such questions await further research. In summary, although middle childhood profiles for the three subtypes of disorganized attachment are emerging, further studies are needed to further trace the trajectories of disorganized and controlling children in the school-age period.

Future Directions: Mediators and Moderators of the Relation Between Attachment and Socioemotional Adaptation in Middle Childhood

The literature just reviewed supports the idea that children with secure attachment relationships have lower risk for maladaptation than their insecure peers. Among insecure groups, children with disorganized/controlling patterns and particularly controlling–punitive forms of interaction are at highest risk, especially with respect to externalizing symptomatology. More research is needed concerning outcomes for other specific insecure groups during this period and with respect to specific externalizing and internalizing symptomatology.

We echo the sentiments of other authors of meta-analyses and review papers (Brumariu & Kerns, 2010; Fearon et al., 2010; Madigan et al., 2012) in emphasizing the need for more research on mediating and moderating processes that might explain associations between different types of insecure attachment and risk outcomes. Several mediating mechanisms related to the internal working model (IWM) construct have been proposed, including more effective emotion regulation capacities (Thompson, 2008) and more positive views of self and other (Wilkinson, 2004). In addition, parent–child interactions remain important as children continue to need parental support as well as models of prosocial behavior and effective emotional communication strategies (Weinfield, Sroufe, Egeland, & Carlson, 2008). Specific aspects of parent–child interactions, such as maintaining a hierarchical structure with parent in control while allowing increasing autonomy, may be particularly important in middle childhood (Dishion & McMahon, 1998). Teacher–child relationships (O'Connor, Collins, & Supplee, 2012; Verschueren, Article 6, this issue), and peer relationships may also mediate associations between attachment and maladaptation in middle childhood.

Several interesting papers have suggested new directions for understanding attachment risk associations in middle childhood. Lecompte and Moss (2014) found that both parent–child interactive role reversal and maternal representations of caregiving helplessness were partial mediators of the relationship between controlling–punitive attachment at early school age and externalizing problems in preadolescence. O'Connor et al. (2012) found that teacher–child relational closeness completely mediated associations between behavioral disorganization and externalizing and internalizing problems in late childhood. Other representational mechanisms, such as child self-esteem, have also been found to play a mediational role in middle childhood, particularly in linking attachment to depression (Lecompte et al., 2014). The mediational role of peer relations in linking attachment to internalizing outcomes has been demonstrated (Bosquet & Egeland, 2006; Brumariu & Kerns, 2013), but much more research on this is needed, given known associations between vulnerable children's affiliations with deviant peers and heightened risk for externalizing problems (Dishion, Nelson, & Bullock, 2004). In summary, these recent works offer interesting avenues to explore in future studies of mediators of attachment risk associations. It is also important to note that, rather than searching for a single causal mechanism that explains the impact of a risk factor, multiple mechanisms, both interactive and representational, are likely to operate in complex chains of influence (Cummings, Davies, & Campbell, 2000).

Some of the most prevalent models of the relation between attachment and risk suggest that the attachment relationship exerts its influence in the context of familial or specific child factors (Cicchetti & Rogosh, 1997; DeKlyen & Greenberg, 2008). Family socioeconomic status, child gender, child clinical status, and genetic markers are among the contextual factors more often included in such models. The diathesis-stress model hypothesizes greater risk for maladaptive outcomes for children in populations of lower socioeconomic status (Lyons-Ruth, Connell, & Grunebaum, 1990). It is interesting that recent meta-analytic results (Fearon et al., 2010; Groh et al., 2012) do not support family adversity (i.e., socioeconomic status) moderation models. However, a few studies suggest that other family variables, such as maternal mental health, marital discord, and stressful life events, may moderate association between attachment and socioemotional problems (Cummings & Davies, 2002; Goodman et al., 2011; Shaw, Owens, Vondra, & Keenan, 1996).

Concerning child moderators, gender differences in the association between attachment and behavior problems have received limited attention in the literature, and results, particularly in middle childhood, tend to be inconsistent (Brumariu & Kerns, 2010). However, some studies show that insecure attachment is more strongly associated with externalizing problems (Fearon et al., 2010) and internalizing problems (Bar-Haim et al., 2007; Madigan et al., 2012) in boys than in girls. Clinical status has also been found to be a significant moderator, in that the association between attachment and externalizing behavior was stronger in clinical versus nonclinical samples (Fearon et al., 2010), and associations with internalizing behavior are stronger in the presence of comorbid externalizing problems (Madigan et al., 2012).

More recently, a few studies have tested the differential susceptibility hypothesis, which suggests that children may vary in their susceptibility to both adverse and beneficial effects of rearing influences (Belsky, Bakermans-Kranenburg, & van Ijzendoorn, 2007). Certain genetic markers, such as the dopamine receptor D4 (DRD4) polymorphism, may reflect variations in temperament and arousal modulation that act as risk factors in the presence of nonoptimal parenting or other environmental conditions leading to externalizing problems in children (Benjamin, Ebstein, & Belmaker, 2002). Associations have been found between early attachment, particularly disorganization, and DRD4 gene polymorphism (Gervai et al., 2005). Other authors found that children are differentially susceptible to insensitive parenting depending on the presence of the 7-repeat DR4 allele (Bakermans-Kranenburg & van Ijzendoorn, 2006). Further research is needed to detail the developmental processes through which such genetic markers interact with attachment in shaping specific externalizing and internalizing behaviors as well as psychopathology in general in middle childhood.

In conclusion, these results support Bowlby's (1969) original idea that attachment processes may well have an integrative and long-term influence on developmental systems crucial to adaptive functioning. They underscore the importance of attachment models in the evaluation and treatment of psychopathology as well as in predicting normative development. These ideas are supported by contemporary research establishing links between attachment and neurodevelopmental processes (Gervai et al., 2005) underlying biological, cognitive, and social behavior as well as the success of attachment-based intervention programs in reducing externalizing problems (Bakermans-Kranenburg, van Ijzendoorn, & Juffer, 2003; Moss et al., 2011). Future studies are needed to detail the specific developmental processes operating in middle childhood that influence long-term and concurrent associations between different types of attachment relationships and specific symptomatology.

References

Ainsworth, M. D. S., Blehar, M. C., Waters, E., & Wall, S. (1978). *Patterns of attachment: A psychological study of the strange situation*. Hillsdale, NJ: Erlbaum.

Bakermans-Kranenburg, M. J., & van Ijzendoorn, M. H. (2006). Gene–environment interaction of the dopamine D4 receptor (DRD4) and observed maternal insensitivity predicting externalizing behavior in preschoolers. *Developmental Psychobiology, 48*, 406–409.

Bakermans-Kranenburg, M. J., van Ijzendoorn, M. H., & Juffer, F. (2003). Less is more: Meta-analyses of sensitivity and attachment interventions in early childhood. *Psychological Bulletin, 129*, 195–215.

Bar-Haim, Y., Dan, O., Eshel, Y., & Sagi-Schwartz, A. (2007). Predicting children's anxiety from early attachment relationships. *Journal of Anxiety Disorders, 21*, 1061–1068.

Belsky, J., Bakermans-Kranenburg, M. J., & van Ijzendoorn, M. H. (2007). For better and for worse: Differential susceptibility to environmental influences. *Current Directions in Psychological Science, 16*, 300–304.

Belsky, J., & Fearon, R. M. P. (2002). Infant–mother attachment security, contextual risk, and early development: A moderational analysis. *Development and Psychopathology, 1*, 293–310.

Benjamin, J., Ebstein, R. P., & Belmaker, R. H. (Eds.). (2002). *Molecular genetics and the human personality*. Washington, DC: American Psychiatric Publishing.

Bosquet, M., & Egeland, B. (2006). The development and maintenance of anxiety symptoms from infancy through adolescence in a longitudinal sample. *Development and Psychopathology, 18*, 517–550.

Bowlby, J. (1969). *Attachment and loss: Vol. 1. Attachment*. New York, NY: Basic Books.

Bowlby, J. (1989). The role of attachment in personality development and psychopathology. In S. I. Greenspan & G. H. Pollock (Eds.), *The course of life: Vol. 1* (pp. 229–270). Madison, CT: International Universities Press.

Brumariu, L. E., & Kerns, K. (2010). Parent–child attachment and internalizing symptoms in childhood and adolescence: A review of empirical findings and future directions. *Development and Psychopathology, 22*, 177–203.

Brumariu, L. E., & Kerns, K. (2013). Pathways to anxiety: Contributions of attachment history, temperament, peer competence, and ability to manage intense emotions. *Child Psychiatry & Human Development, 44*, 504–515.

Brumariu, L. E., Kerns, K., & Seibert, A. (2012). Mother–child attachment, emotion regulation, and anxiety symptoms in middle childhood. *Personal Relationships, 19*, 569–585.

Bureau, J.-F., Easterbrooks, M. A., & Lyons-Ruth, K. (2009). Maternal depressive symptoms in infancy: Unique contribution to children's depressive symptoms in childhood and adolescence? *Development and Psychopathology, 21*, 519–537.

Bureau, J.-F., & Moss, E. (2010). Behavioural precursors of attachment representations in middle childhood and links with child social adaptation. *British Journal of Developmental Psychology, 28*, 657–677.

Cassidy, J., Marvin, R. S., & MacArthur Attachment Working Group. (1992). *Attachment organization in three- and four-year-olds: Procedures and coding manual*. Unpublished manuscript, University of Virginia.

Cicchetti, D., & Rogosh, F. A. (1996). Equifinality and multifinality in developmental psychopathology. *Development and Psychopathology, 8*, 597–600.

Cummings, E. M., & Davies, P. T. (2002). Effects of marital conflict on children: Recent advances and emerging themes in process-oriented research. *Journal of Child Psychology and Psychiatry and Allied Disciplines, 43*, 31–63.

Cummings, E. M., Davies, P. T., & Campbell, S. B. (2000). *Developmental psychopathology and family process: Theory, research, and clinical implications*. New York, NY: Guilford Press.

DeKlyen, M., & Greenberg, M. T. (2008). Attachment and psychopathology in childhood. In J. Cassidy & P. Shaver (Eds.), *Handbook of attachment: Theory, research, and clinical applications* (2nd ed., pp. 637–665). New York, NY: Guilford Press.

Dishion, T. J., & McMahon, R. J. (1998). Parental monitoring and the prevention of child and adolescent problem behavior: A conceptual and empirical formulation. *Clinical Child and Family Psychology Review, 1*, 61–75.

Dishion, T. J., Nelson, S. E., & Bullock, B. M. (2004). Premature adolescent autonomy: Parent disengagement and deviant peer process in the amplification of problem behaviour. *Journal of Adolescence, 27*, 515–530.

Dubois-Comtois, K., Moss, E., Cyr, C., & Pascuzzo, K. (2013). Behavior problems in middle childhood: The predictive role of maternal distress, child attachment, and mother–child interactions. *Journal of Abnormal Child Psychology, 41*, 1311–1324. doi:10.1007/s10802-013-9764-6

Edelbrock, C., Costello, A. J., Dulcan, M. K., Kalas, R., & Conover, N. C. (1985). Age differences in the reliability of the psychiatric interview of the child. *Child Development, 56*, 265–275.

Fearon, R. P., Bakermans-Kranenburg, M. J., van Ijzendoorn, M. H., Lapsley, A.-M., & Roisman, G. I. (2010). The significance of insecure attachment and disorganization in the development of children's externalizing behavior: A meta-analytic study. *Child Development, 81*, 435–456.

Fearon, R. P., & Belsky, J. (2011). Infant–mother attachment and the growth of externalizing problems across the primary school years. *Journal of Child Psychology and Psychiatry, 52*, 782–791.

Gervai, J., Nemoda, Z., Lakatos, K., Ronai, Z., Toth, I., Ney, K., & Sasvari-Szekely, M. (2005). Transmission disequilibrium tests confirm the link between DRD4 gene polymorphism and infant attachment. *American Journal of Medical Genetics Part B, 132B*, 126–130.

Goodman, S. H., Rouse, M. H., Connell, A. M., Broth, M. R., Hall, C. M., & Heyward, D. (2011). Maternal depression and child psychopathology: A meta-analytic review. *Clinical Child and Family Psychology Review, 14*, 1–27.

Groh, A. M., Roisman, G. I., van Ijzendoorn, M. H., Bakermans-Kranenburg, M. J., & Fearon, R. P. (2012). The significance of disorganized attachment for children's internalizing symptoms: A meta-analytic study. *Child Development, 83*, 591–610.

Kerns, K. A. (2008). Attachment in middle childhood. In J. Cassidy & P. R. Shaver (Eds.), *Handbook of attachment* (2nd ed., pp. 366–382). New York, NY: Guilford Press.

Lecompte, V., & Moss, E. (2014). Disorganized and controlling patterns of attachment, role-reversal and caregiving helplessness: Links to adolescents' externalizing problems. *American Journal of Orthopsychiatry, 84*, 581–589.

Lecompte, V., Moss, E., Cyr, C., & Pascuzzo, K. (2014). Preschool attachment, self-esteem and the development of preadolescent anxiety and depressive symptoms. *Attachment & Human Development, 16*, 242–260.

Lyons-Ruth, K., Connell, D. B., & Grunebaum, H. U. (1990). Infants at social risk: Maternal depression and family support services as mediators of infant development and security of attachment. *Child Development, 61*, 85–98.

Lyons-Ruth, K., Easterbrooks, M. A., & Cibelli, C. D. (1997). Infant attachment strategies, infant mental lag, and maternal depressive symptoms: Predictors of internalizing and externalizing problems at age 7. *Developmental Psychology, 33*, 681–692.

Madigan, S., Atkinson, L., Laurin, K., & Benoit, D. (2012). Attachment and internalizing behavior in early childhood: A meta-analysis. *Developmental Psychology, 49*, 1–18.

Main, M., & Cassidy, J. (1988). Categories of response to reunion with the parent at age 6: Predictable from infant attachment classifications and stable over a 1-month period. *Developmental Psychology, 24*, 415–426.

Main, M., & Solomon, J. (1990). *Procedures for identifying infants as disorganized/disoriented during the Ainsworth Strange Situation.* Chicago, IL: University of Chicago Press.

Manassis, K. (2011). Child–parent relations: Attachment and anxiety disorders. In W. K. Silverman & A. P. Field (Eds.), *Anxiety disorders in children and adolescents* (pp. 280–298). Cambridge, UK: Cambridge University Press. doi:10.1017/CBO9780511994920.014

Moss, E., Bureau, J. F., St.-Laurent, D., Cyr, C., & Mongeau, C. (2004). Correlates of attachment at age 3: Construct validity of the preschool attachment classification system. *Developmental Psychology, 40*, 323–334.

Moss, E., Bureau, J.-F., St.-Laurent, D., & Tarabulsy, G. M. (2011). Understanding disorganized attachment at preschool and school age: Examining divergent pathways of disorganized and controlling children. In J. Solomon & C. George (Eds.), *Disorganized attachment and caregiving* (pp. 52–79). New York. NY: Guilford Press.

Moss, E., Cyr, C., Bureau, J.-F., Tarabulsy, G. M., & Dubois-Comtois, K. (2005). Stability of attachment during the preschool period. *Developmental Psychology, 41*, 773–783.

Moss, E., Cyr, C., & Dubois-Comtois, K. (2004). Attachment at early school age and developmental risk: Examining family contexts and behavior problems of controlling–caregiving, controlling–punitive, and behaviorally disorganized children. *Developmental Psychology, 40*, 519–532.

Moss, E., Dubois-Comtois, K., Cyr, C., Tarabulsy, G. M., St.-Laurent, D., & Bernier, A. (2011). Efficacy of a home-visiting intervention aimed at improving maternal sensitivity, child attachment, and behavioral outcomes for maltreated children: A randomized control trial. *Development and Psychopathology, 23*, 195–210.

Moss, E., Pascuzzo, K., & Simard, V. (2012). Treating insecure and disorganized attachments in school-aged children. In K. Nader (Ed.), *School rampage shootings and other youth disturbances: Early preventive interventions* (pp. 127–157). New York, NY: Taylor & Francis.

Moss, E., Smolla, N., Cyr, C., Dubois-Comtois, K., Mazzarello, T., & Berthiaume, C. (2006). Attachment and behavior problems in middle childhood as reported by adult and child informants. *Development and Psychopathology, 18*, 425–444.

Munson, J. A., McMahon, R. J., & Spieker, S. J. (2001). Structure and variability in the developmental trajectory of children's externalizing problems: Impact of infant attachment, maternal depressive symptomatology, and child sex. *Development and Psychopathology, 13*, 277–296.

NICHD Early Child Care Research Network. (2004). Affect dysregulation in the mother–child relationship in the toddler years: Antecedents and consequences. *Development and Psychopathology, 16*, 43–68.

NICHD Early Child Care Research Network. (2006). Infant–mother attachment classification: Risk and protection in relation to changing maternal caregiving quality. *Developmental Psychology, 42*, 38–58.

O'Connor, E., Bureau, J.-F., McCartney, K., & Lyons-Ruth, K. (2011). Risks and outcomes associated with disorganized/controlling patterns of attachment at age three years in the National Institute of Child Health & Human Development study of early child care and youth development. *Infant Mental Health Journal, 32*, 450–472.

O'Connor, E., Collins, B. A., & Supplee, L. (2012). Behavior problems in late childhood: The roles of early maternal attachment and teacher–child relationship trajectories. *Attachment & Human Development, 14*, 265–288.

O'Connor, T. G., & Spagnola, M. E. (2009). Early stress exposure: Concepts, findings, and implications, with particular emphasis on attachment disturbances. *Child and Adolescent Psychiatry and Mental Health, 3.* doi:10.1186/1753-2000-3-24

Shaw, D. S., Owens, E. B., Vondra, J. I., & Keenan, K. (1996). Early risk factors and pathways in the development of early disruptive behavior problems. *Development and Psychopathology, 8*, 679–699.

Solomon, J., George, C., & De Jong, A. (1995). Children classified as controlling at age six: Evidence of disorganized representational strategies and aggression at home and at school. *Development and Psychopathology, 7*, 447–463.

Teti, D. M. (1999). Conceptualizations of disorganization in the preschool years: An integration. In J. Solomon & C. George (Eds.), *Attachment disorganization* (pp. 213–242). New York, NY: Guilford Press.

Thompson, R. A. (2008).*Early attachment and later development: Familiar questions, new answers.* New York, NY: Guilford Press.

Verschueren, K., & Marcoen, A. (1999). Representation of self and socioemotional competence in kindergartners: Differential and combined effects of attachment to mother and father. *Child Development, 70*, 183–201.

Warren, S. L., Huston, L., Egeland, B., & Sroufe, L. A. (1997). Child and adolescent anxiety disorders and early attachment. *Journal of the American Academy of Child & Adolescent Psychiatry, 36*, 637–644. doi:10.1097/00004583-199705000-00014

Weinfield, N. S., Sroufe, L. A., Egeland, B., & Carlson, E. (2008). Individual differences in infant–caregiver attachment. In J. Cassidy & P. R. Shaver (Eds.), *Handbook of attachment: Theory, research, and clinical applications* (pp. 78–101). New York, NY: Guilford Press.

Wilkinson, R. B. (2004). The role of parental and peer attachment in the psychological health and self-esteem of adolescents. *Journal of Youth and Adolescence, 33*, 479–493.

ELLEN MOSS *is a professor at the Université du Québec à Montréal.*

VANESSA LECOMPTE *is a postdoctoral fellow for McGill University.*

Verschueren, K. (2015). Middle childhood teacher–child relationships: Insights from an attachment perspective and remaining challenges. In G. Bosmans & K. A. Kerns (Eds.), *Attachment in middle childhood: Theoretical advances and new directions in an emerging field. New Directions for Child and Adolescent Development, 148,* 77–91.

6

Middle Childhood Teacher–Child Relationships: Insights From an Attachment Perspective and Remaining Challenges

Karine Verschueren

Abstract

An increasing body of research points to the significance of teacher–child relationships in shaping children's development. Extending the research literature on early childhood, this review examines the value of an attachment perspective to the study of teacher–child relationships in middle childhood. First, we discuss the conceptualization and assessment of teacher–child relationship quality from an attachment perspective. Second, we examine how attachment theory guides the search for antecedents at the child and teacher level. Third, we discuss some of the mechanisms that may explain the developmental significance of teacher–child relationships according to attachment theory. Finally, we discuss how attachment theory has inspired interventions to improve teacher–child relationship quality. We conclude that middle childhood has been understudied in attachment-based teacher–child relationship research and that insights from attachment theory and other perspectives need to be combined to progress our understanding of the role of teacher–child relationships in middle childhood. © 2015 Wiley Periodicals, Inc.

I n middle childhood, school becomes an increasingly important context for children's development. Within this context, children form interpersonal relationships not only with their peers but also with their teachers. A growing body of research points to the significance of teacher–child relationships in shaping children's peer experiences as well as their behavioral, emotional, and academic adjustment in schools (e.g., Pianta, Hamre, & Stuhlman, 2003). To conceptualize the quality of teacher–child relationships, scholars have used several models. These include attachment-based models, social support models, socialization models, interpersonal theory, developmental systems models, and social-motivational models. Each provides a complementary perspective on teacher–child relationships, emphasizing the importance of (slightly) different dimensions of teacher–child interactions. The aim of this article is not to give an overview of these models and their evidence (see Davis, 2003; Koomen, Verschueren, & Thijs, 2006; Pianta et al., 2003; Sabol & Pianta, 2012). Instead, consistent with the aim of this issue, I focus exclusively on attachment theory. Attachment theory has made contributions to the conceptualization and operationalization of "high-quality" teacher–child relationships; guided hypotheses regarding the antecedents, consequences, and intervening mechanisms of teacher–child relationship quality; and inspired the development of relationship-focused interventions (Verschueren & Koomen, 2012). Most empirical research supporting the value of an attachment perspective has focused on early childhood (see Sabol & Pianta, 2012, for a recent review). In this article, and aligning with the scope of this issue, I address the question of whether these contributions of attachment theory also apply to middle childhood, and I identify remaining challenges to the study of middle childhood teacher–child relationships.

I first discuss the implications of adopting an attachment framework for the conceptualization of teacher–child relationships in middle childhood. Then I give an overview of attachment-based assessments for this age period. Next, I examine how attachment theory guides the study of antecedents of teacher–child relationship quality as well as its consequents and explaining mechanisms. Then I discuss how attachment theory inspires the development of interventions to improve teacher–child relationship quality. Finally, I outline some conclusions and remaining questions for future research. As the large majority of studies conducted from an attachment perspective focus on the early childhood years, I discuss these findings briefly, referring to extant reviews as much as possible, and then move to implications and findings for middle childhood.

Conceptualization of Teacher–Child Relationships

For a long time, attachment research has focused almost exclusively on parent–child relationships as a context for children's development. In 1992, Robert C. Pianta edited a special issue of this journal, which was titled

Beyond the Parent: The Role of Other Adults in Children's Lives. Ever since this pioneering issue, attachment theory and research have influenced the conceptualization of teacher–child relationships in at least two important ways. First, an attachment perspective highlights the secure base and safe haven function of teachers. Second, it stresses the significance of the affective quality of dyadic teacher–child relationships. These properties of teacher–child relationships are discussed next, focusing on implications for middle childhood.

Teacher as Secure Base and Safe Haven. When adopting an attachment perspective, one of the first questions to ask is whether the teacher–child relationship can be considered an attachment relationship. As argued elsewhere (Verschueren & Koomen, 2012), I contend that most teacher–child relationships cannot be regarded as an attachment bond, defined as a "relatively long-enduring tie in which the partner is important as a unique individual and is interchangeable with none other" (Ainsworth, 1989, p. 711). Teacher–child relationships are usually not exclusive or durable, as in most educational systems children change teachers every school year and children have to share the teacher with many others in the classroom. Moreover, the emotional investment of parents in the relationship with their children is more intense than that of teachers. Relatedly, the primary role of parents is that of caregiver, whereas the primary role of teachers, especially in late elementary school and beyond, is that of instructor (Rimm-Kaufman & Pianta, 2000). Despite this, attachment researchers have argued that teachers can be regarded as temporary or ad hoc attachment figures for children, meaning that they may play the role of a safe haven and a secure base for the children in their classroom (Verschueren & Koomen, 2012; Zajac & Kobak, 2006). This argument implies that children may seek support and comfort from their teacher in times of stress and that the relationship with the teacher may help them to feel more comfortable exploring their learning environment. Several studies in early childhood have supported this assumption (see Verschueren & Koomen, 2012, for a review).

The question is raised whether there is evidence for a similar function of teachers in middle childhood. For younger children, the role of the teacher as an attachment figure may be expected to be of greater importance, because the attachment system of these children gets activated more frequently and their capacity for self-regulation is more limited (Verschueren & Koomen, 2012). It has been argued that children show more diversification of their attachment networks with age (Seibert & Kerns, 2009), implying that they may be more likely to turn to attachment figures beyond parents. Especially in situations in which parents are not available, such as in school settings, alternative adult caregivers might temporarily play the role of attachment figures (Seibert & Kerns, 2009).

In contrast with studies in early childhood, I know of no study to systematically *observe* children's use of the teacher as a safe haven and secure base in middle childhood. Using child interviews, Seibert and Kerns

(2009) investigated the safe haven component of attachment by examining who children seek out in various attachment-relevant situations, including emotion-eliciting situations at school. A sizable number of children spontaneously endorsed going to teachers in these situations, although peers and parents were chosen more often. In a sample of 3- to 12-year-olds, Koomen, Verschueren, Van Schooten, Jak, and Pianta (2012) found that, given the same level of teacher-perceived closeness of the relationship with children, teachers rated older children as likely to seek less comfort when upset than younger children. Thus, as children move into middle childhood, their safe haven behavior may take forms other than overt (physical) comfort seeking from attachment figures. Or, as stated by Kerns (2008), "the goal of the attachment system changes from *proximity* of the attachment figure in early childhood to *availability* of the attachment figure in middle childhood" (p. 367, emphasis in original). In line with these findings, a recent study among early adolescents (grade 7) showed that teachers fulfilled more the role of secure base than of safe haven (De Laet, Colpin, Goossens, Van Leeuwen, & Verschueren, 2014), in that early adolescents strongly endorsed that their teachers encouraged them to try new things and to pursue their goals and future plans, but they relied less on teachers as a source of comfort when upset or worried. The limited safe haven function of teachers was explained by pointing to the increased importance of peers to fulfill functions of safe haven in early adolescence as well as to the increased self-regulating capacities due to major changes in the adolescent brain.

In sum, the limited available findings suggest that the role of teachers as a safe haven becomes less prominent by middle childhood. In contrast, teachers continue to be important as a secure base from which to explore. Moreover, the safe haven function may continue to be important for vulnerable children, such as those with family problems or with self-regulation or emotional problems (e.g., Sabol & Pianta, 2012). In a self-report study in middle childhood, for instance, Lynch and Cicchetti (1992) found that maltreated children reported more psychological proximity seeking than nonmaltreated children, which may indicate a greater reliance on the teacher as a source of comfort and support.

Dyadic and Affective Relationships. Attachment theory and research have influenced the field of teacher–child relationship research in a more general way too, by stressing the significance of the affective quality of dyadic teacher–child relationships. Other models of teacher–child interactions have also outlined the importance of (related dimensions of) emotional support or involvement of teachers. The attachment perspective adds to these models by differentiating between multiple dimensions of affective quality, as described next. Moreover, several models in the field of education, such as interpersonal theory, have conceptualized differences in teacher–child interactions mainly at the class level (e.g., Den Brok, Brekelmans, & Wubbels, 2004). The attachment perspective complements these models by emphasizing that teachers form *specific* relationships with all *individual* children in their class, relationships that vary in affective quality.

In recent years, the affective quality of teacher–child relationships, in both preschool and elementary school, has been defined mostly in terms of the positive relationship dimension of closeness and the negative relationship dimensions of conflict and dependency (Pianta et al., 2003). Research in early childhood samples has convincingly supported the validity of this attachment-based, multidimensional view of student–teacher relationship quality. Fewer studies have included middle childhood samples. In a longitudinal study in which children were followed from kindergarten to sixth grade, Jerome, Hamre, and Pianta (2009) found that average levels of teacher-reported teacher–child conflict increased especially in the early school years, whereas average levels of teacher-reported teacher–child closeness decreased throughout elementary school. Koomen and colleagues (2012) generally confirmed the three-dimensional conceptualization of teacher–child relationship quality from early to late childhood.

Assessment of Teacher–Child Relationships

To assess the role of the teacher as a safe haven and secure base, the Network of Relationships Inventory—Behavioral Systems Version (Furman & Buhrmester, 2009) can be used. This student report scale assesses the extent to which students seek safe haven and secure base support from teachers as well as the extent to which they perceive their teachers as providing a safe haven and secure base for them.

Another, more widely used, scale is the Student-Teacher Relationship Scale (STRS; Pianta, 2001), which measures the three affective relationship dimensions of closeness, conflict, and dependency. Although this teacher rating scale is mostly used in early childhood, it appears to be applicable throughout elementary school (Koomen et al., 2012). The STRS measures the teacher's perspective on the quality of his or her relationship with a specific child, the interactive behavior of the child toward the teacher, and both partners' feelings and thoughts about one another. Teacher-rated relationship quality, indexed by the STRS, was found to relate in predicted ways to observer ratings (e.g., Doumen et al., 2009). These associations are generally moderate, as expected given the differences between "inside" and "outside" perspectives on relationships. Although the STRS was not explicitly introduced as a measure of secure base and safe haven functions of teachers, Verschueren and Koomen (2012) have argued that the dimension of closeness may refer to the degree to which the child uses the teacher as a safe haven and that high scores on dependency may indicate that the child fails to use the teacher as a secure base from which to explore.

Researchers have also probed the child's perspective on the affective quality of the relationship with the teacher. For middle childhood, several validated measures that are framed within an attachment perspective are available. This specification is important because other instruments are also available, but are not framed within an attachment perspective. The Child Appraisal of the Relationship with the Teacher (CARTS; Vervoort, Doumen, & Verschueren, 2014) is a multidimensional measure of the attachment-based dimensions of closeness, conflict, and dependency as perceived by 6- to 10-year-old children. For students in late elementary school, Murray and Zvoch (2011) constructed and validated the Inventory of Teacher-Student Relationships (IT-SR), adapted from the Inventory of Parent and Peer Attachment (IPPA), which assesses three affective dimensions: communication, trust, and alienation. These constructs are considered as consistent with attachment theory, "as they assess students' cognitive representations of the positive and negative affective dimensions of felt security and alienation relationships" (Murray & Zvoch, 2011, p. 501). The People in My Life (PIML; Murray & Greenberg, 2006), also based on the IPPA, differentiates only one positive and one negative teacher–child relationship dimension, namely affiliation and alienation. Finally, also relying on attachment theory but taking a different measurement approach, Harrison, Clarke, and Ungerer (2007) used drawings by 6-year-old children to assess their view on their relationship with the teacher.

Antecedents of Teacher–Child Relationship Quality

Attachment theory and research may also contribute to the field of teacher–child relationships by guiding the search for antecedents of relationship quality. Consistent with Developmental Systems Theory (e.g., O'Connor, 2010; Pianta et al., 2003), scholars have argued that the quality of teacher–child relationships is influenced by the interplay of factors at the child and the teacher level as well as factors in surrounding contexts. With regard to the effects of contextual variables, such as class size, classroom climate, family socioeconomic status, and family–school contact, attachment theory offers less concrete hypotheses. Attachment theory does guide hypotheses regarding antecedents at the level of the child and the teacher.

Child-Level Antecedents. With regard to the child level, a central assumption within an attachment perspective on teacher–child relationships is that the quality of the child's primary attachment to parents is likely to affect the quality of the child's relationship with the teacher (Davis, 2003; O'Connor & McCartney, 2006; Sabol & Pianta, 2012). This relationship continuity may be expected because of several intervening mechanisms. First, the representational models children form of self and others, based on their experiences in their primary attachment relationships, are expected to affect their expectations, behavior, and interpretations in relationships with other caregiving adults. Thus, children who lack trust in the availability of parents are also more likely to lack trust in the availability of teachers.

Other processes may also be at work. For instance, the security of attachment to primary caregivers also affects children's self-regulation, and ample evidence has shown that children who lack self-regulatory capacities in the school context are at increased risk for developing negative relationships with teachers (e.g., Cadima, Verschueren, Leal, & Guedes, in press). Also, parents of secure children may model more appropriate social behavior or may provide their children with more social experiences, thereby facilitating their social skills not only in relationships with peers but also in relationships with adults (see Berlin, Cassidy, & Appleyard, 2008, for these and other possible explaining mechanisms).

Several studies have confirmed this expected relationship continuity in early childhood education settings (e.g., meta-analysis by Ahnert, Pinquart, & Lamb, 2006). As concluded by Sabol and Pianta (2012), these studies have generally shown significant but moderate concordance between parent–child and teacher–child relationship quality, leaving room for the effects of other child, teacher, or contextual characteristics. With regard to teacher–child relationships in middle childhood, O'Connor, Collins, and Supplee (2012) used longitudinal data from the National Institute of Child Health and Human Development Early Child Care Research Network Study of Early Child Care and Youth Development (NICHD SECCYD) to show that insecure mother–child attachment at age 3 (i.e., insecure/other attachment) was associated with increased risk to belong to the "stable low closeness" teacher–child relationship trajectory group from prekindergarten to grade 5. Also, insecure/other children were less likely to belong to the "low-conflict" group. However, associations were modest and were not revealed for the other insecure attachment types (i.e., avoidant, ambivalent, controlling). (See also Jerome et al., 2009.) Most studies have focused on demonstrating relationship continuity rather than on explaining it. It would be interesting for future research to move beyond such a mere demonstration to examine the key explaining mechanisms and how they may possibly differ for various subgroups (e.g., age groups, sexes, risk groups).

Teacher-Level Antecedents. At the teacher level, attachment theory and research highlight the importance of teacher *sensitivity* to children's needs as a central antecedent of relationship quality. Sensitivity has been considered a key proximal determinant of parent–child attachment quality, and its role has been demonstrated in observational as well as intervention research (Bakermans-Kranenburg, van Ijzendoorn, & Juffer, 2003). A meta-analysis by Ahnert and colleagues (2006) confirmed the predictive role of professional caregiver sensitivity for the quality of caregiver–child relationships as well. Whereas caregivers' sensitivity to individual children predicted attachment security only in home-based settings, group-level sensitivity was a predictor of child–caregiver attachment, especially in child care centers. Several studies in early elementary school have also revealed an association between classroom-level teacher sensitivity and the quality of dyadic teacher–child relationships, albeit mostly among children at risk for maladjustment. For example, in a study in first graders, Hamre and Pianta (2005) found that moderate to high levels of observed emotional support (a composite including teacher sensitivity) reduced teacher–child conflict, but only among children displaying high functional risk for school maladjustment. Similarly, Buyse, Verschueren, Doumen, Van Damme, and Maes (2008, Study 2) found no direct association between observed emotional support of teachers (a composite including teacher sensitivity) and the quality of individual relationships, but they did find a protective effect for children with high levels of internalizing or externalizing behavior. It is not clear yet whether these findings generalize to late elementary school.

Combining the assumptions regarding the significance of child attachment history and teacher sensitivity, Buyse, Verschueren, and Doumen (2011) examined the joint effects of mother–child attachment security and teacher sensitivity on teacher-perceived quality of the relationship with the child. Results showed that less secure mother–child attachment related to less closeness in the teacher–child relationship, but only when teacher sensitivity toward the whole class was observed to be low. In the case of high teacher sensitivity, continuity of relationship problems could be counteracted. These findings are promising for practice, as they imply that teachers can redirect the relational development of children with an insecure history of attachment. The study of Buyse and colleagues was conducted among kindergartners, raising the question of whether the teacher's buffering role for insecurely attached children extends to the middle childhood years. In addition, it remains unclear *why* this buffering effect is observed: Does it reflect modifications in children's representational models of relationships? Or rather are the effects of teachers situated at the level of children's self-regulatory capacities or social skills? These are important remaining questions to be addressed.

Grounded in parent–child attachment research, scholars have also begun to consider the teacher's mental representation of the relationship with individual children as an antecedent of relationship quality (Spilt & Koomen, 2009; Stuhlman & Pianta, 2002). To assess these mental representations, they used the Teacher Relationship Interview, a relationship-focused interview, inspired by the Adult Attachment Interview, in which the teacher is asked to reflect on his or her professional role in terms of providing emotional support and socialization and on his or her affective experiences with a specific child. Findings indicate that teachers' narratives, and particularly their narrated affective experiences, are predictive of the quality of their relationships with individual students (Spilt & Koomen, 2009; Stuhlman & Pianta, 2002). Also, intervention research suggests that the quality of the relationship with a student may be fostered by enhancing teachers' reflection on this relationship (Spilt, Koomen, Thijs, & van der Leij, 2012).

In sum, whereas developmental systems theory offers a valuable overarching theoretical framework for studying a multitude of antecedents and their interplay at various levels (e.g., child, teacher, school, neighborhood), attachment theory provides "content" to some of these antecedents, specifically at the level of the child and the teacher. Attachment research has highlighted the long-lasting role of early parent–child attachment for children's relationship formation with teachers across elementary school, but also suggests the potential of teachers to counteract continuity of relationship problems.

Explaining the Developmental Significance of Dyadic Teacher–Child Relationship Quality

Longitudinal and intervention research has demonstrated the importance of high-quality teacher–child relationships in early childhood, as conceptualized within an attachment perspective, for children's school engagement, achievement, and behavioral and emotional adjustment (see Pianta et al., 2003, and Sabol & Pianta, 2012, for reviews). Considering the average decline in the quality of the teacher–child relationship (e.g., Jerome et al., 2009) and the reduced opportunities for one-to-one teacher–child interactions in class (Rimm-Kaufman & Pianta, 2000), the impact of teacher–child relationships on child development may decrease as children move into middle childhood. The limited available longitudinal research, however, does not support this. Maldonado-Carreño and Votruba-Drzal (2011), for instance, found that the beneficial impact of teacher–child relationship quality for child behavioral and academic adjustment did not change as children moved through elementary school. Research from other perspectives (such as social support and motivational models) has yielded similar conclusions (e.g., Hughes, 2011; Roorda, Koomen, Spilt, & Oort, 2011). Another important question is whether positive teacher–child relationships can divert developmental trajectories of children at risk for maladjustment. Several studies have demonstrated the protective effect of close teacher–child relationships for children showing demographic, academic, or behavioral risks for school maladjustment (see Sabol & Pianta, 2012, for an overview). The more limited available research among at-risk students in middle childhood points in the same direction (e.g., Murray & Greenberg, 2006; Murray & Zvoch, 2011).

Scholars have started to study the mechanisms that explain these effects. Different theoretical perspectives point to different possible explaining mechanisms. Socialization models, for instance, highlight the intervening role of children's internalization of school values and goals, whereas motivational models emphasize the mediating role of children's need satisfaction. Attachment theory offers an additional valuable framework. Doumen, Buyse, Colpin, and Verschueren (2011), for instance, tested and confirmed the assumption that negative teacher–child relationships shape children's self-representations, which in turn affect their behavioral development. Additionally, attachment research puts forward that high-quality teacher–child relationships foster children's self-regulation capacities, which in turn improve their adaptive social and academic functioning (Cadima et al., in press; Rimm-Kaufman, Curby, Grimm, Nathanson, & Brock, 2009). Relatedly, and also drawing from attachment theory, Ahnert, Harwardt-Heinecke, Kappler, Eckstein-Madry, and Milatz (2012) showed that children with close, nonconflicted relationships with their teacher showed more optimal stress regulation in terms of cortisol profiles, which may also explain more positive developmental and learning outcomes. In general, few studies have examined mechanisms to explain the well-established effects of teacher–child relationships; thus, testing these mechanisms and possible developmental differences is a fruitful area for future research (Hughes, 2012).

In sum, attachment theory clearly yields interesting hypotheses with regard to the mechanisms that may explain the developmental significance of teacher–child relationships. However, to provide a complete picture of the pathways through which teacher–child relationships impact child development in different domains, other theoretical perspectives are also needed.

Interventions to Improve Dyadic Teacher–Child Relationship Quality

Evidence that child development in school is promoted when the teacher is sensitive to the child's social and emotional needs has inspired interventions and teacher training programs (see Sabol & Pianta, 2012, for an overview). Banking Time (Driscoll & Pianta, 2010), for instance, aims at improving teachers' sensitivity and affective teacher–child relationship quality by organizing one-on-one child-directed sessions. Building on this and other related interventions (e.g., McIntosh, Rizza, & Bliss, 2000), Playing-2-Gether (Vancraeyveldt et al., 2015) combines attachment theory and learning theory with the aim of improving both affective teacher–child relationship quality and teachers' behavioral management. Although these interventions have targeted preschool children, the core attachment-based principles (e.g., conveying acceptance and sensitivity) may also extend to middle childhood.

Murray and Malmgren (2005) developed a teacher–student relationship program with the purpose of establishing involvement, communication, and warmth of teachers with adolescents who show behavioral and emotional problems in a high-risk socioeconomic context. Teachers/mentors and students have weekly one-on-one meetings, and teachers are instructed to communicate positive feedback and high expectations and to establish a personal relationship with students. The intervention is based, in part, on the Check & Connect intervention model (Anderson, Christenson, Sinclair, & Lehr, 2004), which has been developed to promote student engagement with school through continuously checking indicators of student engagement and establishing nurturing, supportive, and continuing connections (connecting) with the students, families, and school staff. Although these programs include ideas from attachment-based teacher–child relationship literature, they also include components derived from other theories (e.g., on student motivation and engagement). This broadened perspective is understandable in light of the generally stronger emphasis on academics as children progress in school and the general increase of academic problems, such as disengagement, especially among socially disadvantaged groups.

Conclusions and Remaining Questions

Attachment research has traditionally focused almost exclusively on parent–child attachment relationships in the home environment. In the past two decades, an increasing body of literature has suggested that teacher–child relationships and children's functioning at school also constitute fruitful areas for attachment research. This article addressed the potential contribution of attachment theory and research to the study of teacher–child relationships in middle childhood, a developmental period has been understudied in attachment-based teacher–child relationship research. Nevertheless, attachment theory seems to offer a fruitful framework for further research in this area.

First, attachment theory highlights the importance of affective, dyadic relationships between teachers and individual children, offering a differentiated, multidimensional conceptual model and related assessments. Also, it highlights the importance of the teacher as a secure base from which children can explore the learning environment, and it may inspire researchers to address (normative) developmental aspects of the safe haven function of teachers: How do older children signal their need for teacher support? Which teacher behaviors are considered key aspects of teacher availability in middle childhood? Do children need their teacher less as a safe haven as they move into middle childhood, or does their security-seeking behavior merely take a different form?

Second, attachment theory provides a theoretical and empirical basis for hypotheses regarding antecedents and consequences of teacher–child relationship quality, and, even more important, explaining mechanisms or pathways. Extending promising findings in early childhood, we should further investigate if and under what conditions teacher sensitivity continues to buffer the relational functioning of at-risk children in the middle childhood years and possible boundaries of these protective effects (e.g., due to severity of the child's problems).

Third, attachment theory has inspired researchers to develop relationship-focused interventions in schools, and promising findings in early childhood may stimulate researchers to invest in programs for middle childhood. As the focus on academics typically increases in upper elementary education, convincing teachers and schools to invest in interpersonal resources may be challenging. However, ample research has shown a link between social relationships in school and children's academic engagement and achievement, demonstrating the importance of targeting these resources.

This review also made clear that to study teacher–child relationships in middle childhood, we need other, complementary conceptual frameworks as well. For example, motivational models highlight the importance of additional relationship dimensions, such as structure or autonomy support; interpersonal theory points to the importance of teacher–child interactions at the class level; and developmental systems theory provides a comprehensive model to study multiple antecedent factors at different levels. By combining insights and hypotheses from attachment-based models with other theoretical perspectives, our understanding of the role of teacher–child relationships in middle childhood will likely progress significantly.

References

Ahnert, L., Harwardt-Heinecke, E., Kappler, G., Eckstein-Madry, T., & Milatz, A. (2012). Student–teacher relationships and classroom climate in first grade: How do they relate to stress reactivity and regulation? *Attachment and Human Development, 14*, 249–263.

Ahnert, L., Pinquart, M., & Lamb, M. E. (2006). Security of children's relationships with nonparental care providers: A meta-analysis. *Child Development, 77*, 664–679.

Ainsworth, M. D. S. (1989). Attachments beyond infancy. *American Psychologist, 44*, 709–716.

Anderson, A. R., Christenson, S. L., Sinclair, M. F., & Lehr, C. A. (2004). Check & connect: The importance of relationships for promoting engagement with school. *Journal of School Psychology, 42*, 95–113.

Bakermans-Kranenburg, M. J., van Ijzendoorn, M. H., & Juffer, F. (2003). Less is more: Meta-analyses of sensitivity and attachment interventions in early childhood. *Psychological Bulletin, 129*, 195–215.

Berlin, L. J., Cassidy, J., & Appleyard, K. (2008). The influence of early attachments on other relationships. In J. Cassidy & P. R. Shaver (Eds.), *Handbook of attachment: Theory, research, and clinical applications* (2nd ed., pp. 333–347). New York, NY: Guilford Press.

Buyse, E., Verschueren, K., & Doumen, S. (2011). Preschoolers' attachment to mother and risk for adjustment problems in kindergarten: Can teachers make a difference? *Social Development, 20*, 33–50.

Buyse, E., Verschueren, K., Doumen, S., Van Damme, J., & Maes, F. (2008). Classroom problem behavior and teacher–child relationships in kindergarten: The moderating role of classroom climate. *Journal of School Psychology, 46*, 367–391.

Cadima, J., Verschueren, K., Leal, T., & Guedes, C. (in press). Teacher–child interactions, teacher–child relationships, and self-regulation in socially disadvantaged young children. *Journal of Abnormal Child Psychology*.

Davis, H. A. (2003). Conceptualizing the role and influence of student–teacher relationships on children's social and cognitive development. *Educational Psychologist, 38,* 207–234.

De Laet, S., Colpin, H., Goossens, L., Van Leeuwen, K., & Verschueren, K. (2014). Comparing parent–child and teacher–child relationships in early adolescence: Measurement invariance of perceived attachment-related dimensions. *Journal of Psychoeducational Assessment, 32,* 521–532.

Den Brok, P., Brekelmans, M., & Wubbels, T. (2004). Interpersonal teacher behaviour and student outcomes. *School Effectiveness and School Improvement, 14*(3–4), 407–442.

Doumen, S., Buyse, E., Colpin, H., & Verschueren, K. (2011). Teacher–child conflict and aggressive behavior in first grade: The intervening role of children's self-esteem. *Infant and Child Development, 20,* 449–465.

Doumen, S., Verschueren, K., Buyse, E., De Munter, S., Max, K., & Moens, L. (2009). Further examination of the convergent and discriminant validity of the Student-Teacher Relationship Scale. *Infant and Child Development, 18,* 502–520.

Driscoll, K. C., & Pianta, R. C. (2010). Banking time in Head Start: Early efficacy of an intervention designed to promote supportive teacher–child relationships. *Early Education and Development, 21,* 38–64.

Furman, W., & Buhrmester, D. (2009). The Network of Relationships Inventory: Behavioral systems version. *International Journal of Behavioral Development, 33,* 470–478. doi:10.1177/0165025409342634

Hamre, B. K., & Pianta, R. C. (2005). Can instructional and emotional support in the first grade classroom make a difference for children at risk of school failure? *Child Development, 76*(5), 949–967. doi:10.1111/j.1467-8624.2005.00889.x

Harrison, L. J., Clarke, L., & Ungerer, J. A. (2007). Children's drawings provide a new perspective on teacher–child relationship quality and school adjustment. *Early Childhood Research Quarterly, 22,* 55–71.

Hughes, J. N. (2011). Longitudinal effects of teachers and student perceptions of teacher–student relationship qualities on academic adjustment. *Elementary School Journal, 112,* 38–60.

Hughes, J. N. (2012). Teacher–student relationships and school adjustment: Progress and remaining challenges. *Attachment & Human Development, 14,* 319–327.

Jerome, E. M., Hamre, B. K., & Pianta, R. C. (2009). Teacher–child relationships from kindergarten to sixth grade: Early childhood predictors of teacher-perceived conflict and closeness. *Social Development, 18,* 915–945. doi:10.1111/j.1467-9507.2008.00508.x

Kerns, K. A. (2008). Attachment in middle childhood. In J. Cassidy & P. R. Shaver (Eds.), *Handbook of attachment: Theory, research, and clinical applications* (2nd ed., pp. 366–382). New York, NY: Guilford Press.

Koomen, H. M. Y., Verschueren, K., & Thijs, J. T. (2006). Assessing aspects of the teacher–child relationship: A critical ingredient of a practice-oriented psychodiagnostic approach. *Educational and Child Psychology, 23,* 50–60.

Koomen, H. M. Y., Verschueren, K., Van Schooten, E., Jak, S., & Pianta, R. (2012). Validating the Student–Teacher Relationship Scale: Testing factor structure and measurement invariance across child gender and age in a Dutch sample. *Journal of School Psychology, 50,* 215–234.

Lynch, M., & Cicchetti, D. (1992). Maltreated children' reports of relatedness to their teachers. In R. C. Pianta (Ed.), *New Directions for Child Development: No. 57. Beyond the parent: The role of other adults in children's lives* (pp. 81–107). San Francisco, CA: Jossey Bass.

Maldonado-Carreño, C., & Votruba-Drzal, E. (2011). Teacher–child relationships and the development of academic and social skills during elementary school: A within and between child analysis. *Child Development, 82,* 601–616.

McIntosh, D. E., Rizza, M. G., & Bliss, L. (2000). Implementing empirically supported interventions: Teacher–child interaction therapy. *Psychology in the Schools, 37*, 453–462.

Murray, C., & Greenberg, M. T. (2006). Examining the importance of social relationships and social contexts in the lives of children with high-incidence disabilities. *Journal of Special Education, 39*, 220–233.

Murray, C., & Malmgren, K. (2005). Implementing a teacher–student relationship program in a high poverty urban school: Effects on social, emotional, and academic adjustment and lessons learned. *Journal of School Psychology, 43*, 137–152.

Murray, C., & Zvoch, K. (2011). The Inventory of Teacher-Student Relationships: Factor structure, reliability, and validity among African American youth in low-income urban schools. *Journal of Early Adolescence, 31*, 493–525.

O'Connor, E. (2010). Teacher–child relationships as dynamic systems. *Journal of School Psychology, 48*, 187–218.

O'Connor, E., Collins, B. A., & Supplee, L. (2012). Behavior problems in late childhood: The roles of early maternal attachment and teacher–child relationship trajectories. *Attachment & Human Development, 14*, 265–288.

O'Connor, E., & McCartney, K. (2006). Testing associations between mother–child and teacher–child relationships. *Journal of Educational Psychology, 26*, 301–326.

Pianta, R. C. (Ed.). (1992). *New Directions for Child Development: No. 57. Beyond the parent: The role of other adults in children's lives*. San Francisco, CA: Jossey-Bass.

Pianta, R. C. (2001). *STRS: Student-Teacher Relationship Scale: Professional manual*. Odessa, FL: Psychological Assessment Resources.

Pianta, R. C., Hamre, B., & Stuhlman, M. (2003). Relationships between teachers and children. In W. M. Reynolds, G. E. Miller, & I. B. Weiner (Eds.), *Handbook of psychology. Vol. 7. Educational psychology* (pp. 199–234). Hoboken, NJ: Wiley.

Rimm-Kaufman, S. E., Curby, T. W., Grimm, K. J., Nathanson, L., & Brock, L. (2009). The contribution of children's self-regulation and classroom quality to children's adaptive behaviors in the kindergarten classroom. *Developmental Psychology, 45*(4), 958–972.

Rimm-Kaufman, S. E., & Pianta, R. C. (2000). Teachers' judgments of problems in the transition to kindergarten. *Early Childhood Research Quarterly, 15*, 147–166.

Roorda, D. L., Koomen, H. M. Y., Spilt, J. L., & Oort, F. J. (2011). The influence of affective teacher-student relationships on students' school engagement and achievement: A meta-analytic approach. *Review of Educational Research, 81*, 493–529.

Sabol, T. J., & Pianta, R. C. (2012). Recent trends in research on teacher–child relationships. *Attachment & Human Development, 14*, 213–231.

Seibert, A. C., & Kerns, K. A. (2009). Attachment figures in middle childhood. *International Journal of Behavioral Development, 33*, 347–355.

Spilt, J. L., & Koomen, H. M. Y. (2009). Widening the view on teacher–child relationships: Teachers' narratives concerning disruptive versus nondisruptive children. *School Psychology Review, 38*, 86–101.

Spilt, J. L., Koomen, H. M. Y., Thijs, J. T., & van der Leij, A. (2012). Supporting teachers' relationships with disruptive children: The potential of relationship-focused reflection. *Attachment & Human Development, 14*, 305–318.

Stuhlman, M. W., & Pianta, R. C. (2002). Teachers' narratives about their relationships with children: Associations with behavior in classrooms. *School Psychology Review, 31*, 148–163.

Vancraeyveldt, C., Verschueren, K., Wouters, S., Van Craeyevelt, S., Van Den Noortgate, W., & Colpin, H. (2015). Improving teacher–child relationship quality and teacher-rated behavioral adjustment amongst externalizing preschoolers: Effects of a two-component intervention. *Journal of Abnormal Child Psychology, 43*, 243–257.

Verschueren, K., & Koomen, H. (2012). Teacher–child relationships from an attachment perspective. *Attachment & Human Development, 14*, 205–211.

Vervoort, N., Doumen, S., & Verschueren, K. (2014). Children's appraisal of their relationship with the teacher: Preliminary evidence for construct validity. *European Journal of Developmental Psychology*, *12*, 243–260. doi:10.1080/17405629.2014.989984

Zajac, K., & Kobak, R. (2006). Attachment. In G. G. Bear & K. M. Minke (Eds.), *Children's needs III: Development, prevention and intervention* (pp. 379–389). Washington, DC: National Association of School Psychologists.

KARINE VERSCHUEREN *is a full professor at the research unit School Psychology and Child and Adolescent Development at the Catholic University of Leuven (KU Leuven), Belgium.*

7

Commentary—Culture and Attachment During Middle Childhood

Bin-Bin Chen

Abstract

*Culture has an important impact on attachment. This commentary highlights
three aspects about culture and attachment in middle childhood: (1) the need to
have a more sophisticated consideration of the implication of cultural values,
(2) the need to incorporate the role of societal or political ecological contexts,
and (3) the need to solve the cross-cultural issues in measures. © 2015 Wiley
Periodicals, Inc.*

Support for the preparation of this commentary was provided by the Shanghai Plan-
ning Project of Philosophy and Social Sciences (No. 2013JJY002), China, and a
research fund of the School of Social Development and Public Policy at Fudan University. Correspondence regarding this manuscript should be addressed to Bin-Bin Chen at
chenbinbin@fudan.edu.cn.

I n the past two decades, literature on attachment during middle childhood has developed rapidly (Kerns, 2008; see also Bosmans & Kerns, Article 1, this issue). Despite its tremendous growth, studies have been largely confined to Western contexts. Surprisingly little is known about whether basic findings about attachment in middle childhood found in Western cultures hold within non-Western cultural heritages. Although Bowlby (1969) theorized about the evolutionary design of attachment (see also Del Giudice, Article 2, this issue), suggesting that the formation of an attachment bond is universal regardless of specific cultural contexts, the development of attachment also depends on particular cultural contexts of historical, social, political, and economic factors (Rothbaum, Weisz, Pott, Miyake, & Morelli, 2000; van Ijzendoorn & Sagi-Schwartz, 2008). This commentary discusses three aspects of culture and attachment in middle childhood that have been ignored in previous research. Briefly, these are: (1) the need to have a more sophisticated consideration of the implication of cultural values, (2) the need to incorporate the role of societal or political ecological contexts, and (3) the need to solve the cross-cultural issues in measures.

Cultural Values

One way to define the cultural differences is in terms of the difference between two cultural syndromes—individualism and collectivism (Triandis, 1995). Within individualistic cultural contexts, people place relatively greater emphasis on independence and autonomy. In contrast, within collectivistic cultural contexts, people place greater weight on interdependence and relational harmony (Oyserman, Coon, & Kemmelmeier, 2002; Triandis, 1995). Individualistic and collectivistic values may influence the development of the attachment behavioral system. Unfortunately, there is no empirical evidence to test cross-cultural differences in attachment during middle childhood. From a cross-cultural perspective (e.g., Miyake, Chen, & Campos, 1985), it is predicted that children in collectivistic societies may have a higher rate of anxious attachment and a lower rate of avoidant attachment than their counterparts in individualistic societies.

Although Western literature has indicated that positive parenting behaviors are associated with secure attachment and negative parenting behaviors are associated with insecure attachment (e.g., Karavasilis, Doyle, & Markiewicz, 2003), some negative parenting behaviors may not be related to insecure attachment in non-Western cultures. For example, a study based on a Puerto Rican sample in infancy showed that controlling–caregiving, as characterized by greater valuing of well-behaved behaviors, was related to secure attachment (Carlson & Harwood, 2003). Notably, "tiger mom" or authoritarian parenting is especially evident in Asian parents who emphasize achievement and appropriate/respectful social behaviors. These parenting behaviors have been found to be associated with academic success and socioemotional well-being (Chao & Tseng, 2002). Therefore, future studies that include a variety of culture-specific parental practices may enhance our understanding of the underlying association between parenting and secure attachment. In addition, less research is available on cultural universality of the role of teacher behaviors on teacher–child attachment (see Verschueren, Article 6, this issue). But as found in the parenting area, it may be expected that authoritarian teachers who emphasize achievement and appropriate behaviors may promote the formation of high-quality teacher–child relationships in non-Western cultures where these practices are considered normative.

Cross-cultural differences may exist not only in the distribution of attachment classification and the precursors (e.g., parenting) of attachment but also in the patterns of relationships between attachment and outcomes that were discussed in this issue, including information processing (Zimmermann & Iwanski, Article 4), emotion regulation (Brumariu, Article 3), and psychopathology (Moss & Lecompte, Article 5). Given that it is more important for children in collectivistic societies to have close relationships, avoidant attachment that violates the basic expectations of collectivistic cultures may cause children to be especially at risk for socioemotional difficulties. In contrast, given that autonomy and independence are encouraged in individualistic societies, anxious attachment that violates the basic expectations of individualistic cultures may cause children to be especially at risk for socioemotional difficulties. Therefore, the literature on individualistic and collectivistic values may provide a useful source for hypotheses about attachment patterns and their correlates. From the cross-cultural perspective, three interesting hypotheses described in articles in this issue, which may need to be modified to be culture specific, may be tested in the future.

1. Insecurely attached children may be more sensitive in processing information or stimuli related to social relationships in collectivistic cultures than in individualistic cultures.
2. Securely attached children may be more likely to employ adaptive emotion regulation strategies in collectivistic cultures than in individualistic cultures.
3. Children with controlling–punitive attachment may be at greater risk for increased externalizing problems in individualistic cultures than in collectivistic cultures.

In addition, globalization and social change may result in cultural variation within a society. For example, many Asian countries or areas have encountered great social and economic transformation in which the Western individualistic values have been introduced and integrated into traditional collectivistic values. Consequently, their social contexts have been characterized by a form of cultural mixture (Oyserman et al., 2002). Therefore, in addition to simple comparison between countries, it is necessary to assess the individual cultural orientation within a society and to examine how the cultural orientation, especially at the individual/family level, may influence the attachment system.

Societal or Political Ecological Context

The level of risk in a societal or political context in a particular historical time often reflects long-term traumatic and stressful life events that may influence the attachment behavioral system (Bowlby, 1980). For example, in many underdeveloped or developing countries, such as China, the Philippines, and Mexico, large-scale internal or international migration of parents for better jobs and/or income to other cities or to foreign countries has resulted in leaving their own children behind. According to attachment theory, parental separation has aversive long-term consequences on attachment. Therefore, future studies should test how migratory separation and care by alternative attachment figures may influence the establishment and development of attachment relationships during middle childhood.

Political violence is another example. In the context of continuing political violence, parents may be more likely to have exaggerated overprotectiveness and impaired sensitivity to children's attachment signals, which may in turn lead to the development of ambivalent attachment. This hypothesis was supported by evidence in Israeli infants (van Ijzendoorn & Sagi-Schwartz, 2008) but not in Israeli middle childhood children (Granot & Mayseless, 2001). It remains unclear whether age or increased coping skills (e.g., emotional regulation as discussed by Brumariu, Article 3, this issue) in middle childhood buffer against the role of risk in the societal or political ecological context. Future studies to investigate these questions are needed to enhance our understanding of the processes by which ecological contexts exercise their influence.

Cross-Cultural Issues in Measures

In the past two decades, many Western-based measurement instruments for assessing attachment during middle childhood have been developed (see Bosmans & Kerns, Article 1, this issue). Most of these measures have proved reliable and valid (Dwyer, 2005; Kerns, Schlegelmilch, Morgan, & Abraham, 2005). Some have been used in non-Western societies, such as Argentina (Richaud de Minzi, 2006), China (Chen, 2012; Chen & Chang, 2012), and Korea (Moon, 2009). However, cross-cultural psychometric properties of these instruments have yet to be demonstrated. Like the cross-cultural debate on the validity of attachment measures (e.g., the Strange Situation Procedure [SSP]) in infancy and early childhood (Rothbaum et al., 2000; van Ijzendoorn & Sagi-Schwartz, 2008), the use of Western-based measures of attachment during middle childhood is problematic in

NEW DIRECTIONS FOR CHILD AND ADOLESCENT DEVELOPMENT • DOI: 10.1002/cad

non-Western societies. For example, Richaud de Minzi (2006) omitted items concerning communication quality in the Kerns Security Scale "because they were not consistent in the Argentine sample" (p. 194). Although the author did not clarify why these items were not consistent, it might be due to the different cultural meaning endorsed in Argentine culture. In addition, increased emphasis on the Western individualism orientation reflected in the Western-based measures of attachment (Rothbaum et al., 2000) may limit the sensitivity of such measures among children and attachment figures who have a more collectivism interpersonal orientation. Therefore, in order to avoid misusing assessments and making culturally biased conclusions, it is necessary to first consider whether these instruments are culturally sensitive and psychometrically acceptable for use among children and families whose cultural backgrounds are different from those of the original norm samples (Geisinger, 1994; Marsella & Leong, 1995).

This cultural issue should also be considered for the model of measurement approaches to attachment in middle childhood proposed by Bosmans and Kerns (Article 1, this issue). They argued that all measurement strategies may share a connection with the underlying secure base script. But the connection strength between measurement strategies and an underlying secure base script may vary across cultural contexts. For example, recent research has shown that China was highest in socially desirable responding among nine countries (Bornstein et al., 2015). Thus, is it possible that explicit report may less accurately reflect underlying secure base script in Chinese contexts than other cultural context? It will be interesting to test this model across cultures.

References

Bornstein, M. H., Putnick, D. L., Lansford, J. E., Pastorelli, C., Skinner, A. T., Sorbring, E., … Oburu, P. (2015). Mother and father socially desirable responding in nine countries: Two kinds of agreement and relations to parenting self-reports. *International Journal of Psychology*. doi:10.1002/ijop.12084

Bowlby, J. (1969). *Attachment and loss. Vol. 1. Attachment*. New York, NY: Basic Books.

Bowlby, J. (1980). *Attachment and loss. Vol. 3. Loss: Sadness and depression*. New York, NY: Basic Books.

Carlson, V. J., & Harwood, R. L. (2003). Attachment, culture, and the caregiving system: The cultural patterning of everyday experiences among Anglo and Puerto Rican mother–infant pairs. *Infant Mental Health Journal, 24*, 53–73.

Chao, R., & Tseng, V. (2002). Parenting of Asians. In M. H. Bornstein (Ed.), *Handbook of parenting* (2nd ed., Vol. 4, pp. 59–93). Mahwah, NJ: Erlbaum.

Chen, B.-B. (2012). The association between self-reported mother–child attachment and social initiative and withdrawal in Chinese school-aged children. *Journal of Genetic Psychology, 173*, 279–301.

Chen, B.-B., & Chang, L. (2012). Adaptive insecure attachment and resource control strategies during middle childhood. *International Journal of Behavioral Development, 36*, 389–397.

Dwyer, K. M. (2005). The meaning and measurement of attachment in middle and late childhood. *Human Development, 48*, 155–182.

Geisinger, K. F. (1994). Cross-cultural normative assessment: Translation and adaptation issues influencing the normative interpretation of assessment instruments. *Psychological Assessment*, 6, 304–312.

Granot, D., & Mayseless, O. (2001). Attachment security and adjustment to school in middle childhood. *International Journal of Behavioral Development*, 25, 530–541.

Karavasilis, L., Doyle, A. B., & Markiewicz, D. (2003). Associations between parenting style and attachment to mother in middle childhood and adolescence. *International Journal of Behavioral Development*, 27, 153–164.

Kerns, K. A. (2008). Attachment in middle childhood. In J. Cassidy & P. R. Shaver (Eds.), *Handbook of attchment: Theory, research, and clinical applications* (2nd ed., pp. 366–382). New York, NY: Guilford Press.

Kerns, K. A., Schlegelmilch, A., Morgan, T. A., & Abraham, M. M. (2005). Assessing attachment in middle childhood. In K. A. Kerns & R. A. Richardson (Eds.), *Attachment in middle childhood* (pp. 46–70). New York, NY: Guilford Press.

Marsella, A. J., & Leong, F. T. L. (1995). Cross-cultural issues in personality and career assessment. *Journal of Career Assessment*, 3, 202–218.

Miyake, K., Chen, S.-J., & Campos, J. J. (1985). Infant temperament, mother's mode of interaction, and attachment in Japan: An interim report. *Monographs of the Society for Research in Child Development*, 50, 276–297.

Moon, S.-H. (2009). Relationship of peer relationships, perceived parental rearing attitudes, self-reported attachment security, to loneliness in upper elementary school-age children. *Journal of Korean Academy of Nursing*, 39, 401–408.

Oyserman, D., Coon, H. M., & Kemmelmeier, M. (2002). Rethinking individualism and collectivism: Evaluation of theoretical assumptions and meta-analyses. *Psychological Bulletin*, 128, 3–72.

Richaud de Minzi, M. C. (2006). Loneliness and depression in middle and late childhood: The relationship to attachment and parental styles. *Journal of Genetic Psychology*, 167, 189–210.

Rothbaum, F., Weisz, J., Pott, M., Miyake, K., & Morelli, G. (2000). Attachment and culture: Security in the United States and Japan. *American Psychologist*, 55, 1093–1104.

Triandis, H. C. (1995). *Individualism and collectivism*. Boulder, CO: Westview Press.

van Ijzendoorn, M. H., & Sagi-Schwartz, A. (2008). Cross-cultural patterns of attachment: Universal and contextual dimensions. In J. Cassidy & P. R. Shaver (Eds.), *Handbook of attachment: Theory, research, and clinical applications* (2nd ed., pp. 880–905). New York, NY: Guilford Press.

BIN-BIN CHEN is an assistant professor of psychology at Fudan University, Shanghai, China.

Steele, H. (2015). Commentary—Attachment in middle childhood: Looking back, forward, and within. In G. Bosmans & K. A. Kerns (Eds.), *Attachment in middle childhood: Theoretical advances and new directions in an emerging field*. New Directions for Child and Adolescent Development, 148, 99–104.

8

Commentary—Attachment in Middle Childhood: Looking Back, Forward, and Within

Howard Steele

Abstract

This commentary discusses the articles that comprise this special issue on attachment in middle childhood. Central to this discussion is the distinction between verbal, strategic, and conscious responses to questionnaires as compared to verbal and nonverbal, automatic and largely unconscious responses to interviews. Both methods have been developed to study attachment in middle childhood, often leading to divergent results. Research going forward should include both types of methods in order to maximize the potential for meaningful research and effective clinical work. Ongoing issues of importance for the field include the need to take account of differential susceptibility theory, culture-specific influences, and possible gender differences. This commentary is organized into three sections—looking within, looking behind, and looking ahead—a tripartite distinction that reflects developmental as well as theoretical and applied perspectives vital to hold in mind when researching attachment in middle childhood. © 2015 Wiley Periodicals, Inc.

What lies behind us, and what lies ahead of us are tiny matters compared to what lies within.
—Attributed to various authors, including Oliver Wendell Holmes, Henry David Thoreau, Ralph Waldo Emerson, and an unnamed Wall Street trader

T his commentary addresses issues that arise in the study of attachment during middle childhood by looking within, looking behind, and considering what lies ahead for research into this vital preadolescent, post–early childhood period of life.

Looking Within

The epigraph draws attention to the vital importance of the inner world of emotion regulation, thoughts and feelings about who can be trusted, and fundamental coping abilities—the stuff of middle childhood that is the focus of many of the contributions to this fine issue. At the heart of attachment theory is the fundamental assumption that when attachments are going well, psychological health in general is also to be found (Brumariu, Article 3; Moss & Lecompte, Article 5, both this issue).

During the middle childhood years, we become increasingly capable of making social and psychological judgments underpinned by growing metacognitive skills. Attachment research demonstrates that this understanding of mind and emotion is advanced or precocious in children with a history of secure attachments to primary caregivers (Zimmermann & Iwanski, Article 4, this issue). This issue reveals advances in attachment research in middle childhood and the corresponding goal of understanding and promoting psychological well-being in these important years.

The issue reflects diverse perspectives, including reviews of theory and evidence on emotional regulation in middle childhood (Bumariu, Article 3, this issue), the relevance of evolutionary and biological perspectives (Del Giudice, Article 2, this issue), the processing of social or emotional information (Zimmermann & Iwanski, Article 4, this issue), with consideration of both typical and clinical or atypical pathways (Moss & Lecompte, Article 5, this issue). In addition, the extent to which the teacher–child relationship may be seen as an attachment relationship is considered (Verschueren, Article 6, this issue). To the extent that children see teachers as bigger, stronger, and wiser than they see themselves and also to the extent that they rely on them as a secure base or safe haven, then teachers may be considered attachment figures—but this is much less likely to be the case as children advance through middle childhood toward adolescence.

Article 1 by Bosmans and Kerns provides a useful road map to understand contributions to date and directions that researchers may follow going forward (echoed in diverse and overlapping ways by all other contributions to this issue). Most valuable, perhaps, is their reliance on the dual theory perspective that contrasts strategic (conscious) with automatic (unconscious) processing of information. This distinction serves as way of acknowledging, and valuing, the different research perspectives on attachment in middle childhood—that is, those that rely on questionnaires completed by youth, parents, peers, or teachers, and those that rely on interviews collected from youth themselves, parents, teachers, or others vitally involved in the child's life. With the former method, researchers rely on deliberate or conscious self-reported responses to the carefully conceived language of *others* as it appears on questionnaires (e.g., the Security Scale) or questionnaires tapping into emotion regulation strategies. In contrast, some interview methodologies (Child Attachment Interview [CAI], Friends and Family Interview, or Late CAI—see Article 4) are based on the Adult Attachment Interview (AAI) and are aligned with it in the aim of surprising the unconscious and thereby accessing the inner world of the developing self. Correspondingly, the FFI has, in longitudinal work with low-risk, typically developing children, been associated (backward) to infant–mother and infant–father attachment and to parents' responses to the AAI (Steele & Steele, 2005). In this sense, it appears that automatic unconscious emotion regulation strategies, operative in infancy (and observable in the Strange Situation Procedure [SSP]), may remain more or less stable through 12 years of age when children's development follows a typical trajectory and when interviews are used to tap into these attachment strategies in middle childhood. Interview questions of most relevance appear to be ones that challenge children to think about emotional distress and ambivalent or mixed feelings, for example, "What do you do when you are upset?" and "What do you like most, and what do you like least" in relation to self, peers, siblings, and parents. Questions such as these capture automatic (unconscious) strategies as opposed to deliberate (and conscious) verbal responses (which are better captured via questionnaires). Different information typically arises from each method. Importantly, as Bosmans and Kerns emphasize, both types of information are relevant, and the experience of completing a survey is, like the interview, an experience that foretells many later encounters (e.g., job interviews), so it is good preparation for the future. In addition, with respect to mental health problems or the experience of adversity, a questionnaire is often a productive and nonthreatening way of eliciting information from a youth (who may otherwise be governed by shame and lead to underreporting of experiences of adversity). The sooner we can identify young people in middle childhood who are experiencing attachment insecurities or mental health troubles, the earlier a remedy can be sought (via therapeutic work with parents, pediatricians, or schools) and found, as problems that emerge in middle childhood often continue into adulthood.

Looking Behind

Attachment during infancy and early childhood is readily observable, by way of seeing and hearing how children behave on reunion following an actual (Ainsworth, Blehar, Waters, & Wall, 1978) or imagined separation, as in story stems depicting a dilemma when the child is asked "Show me and tell me what happens next." The SSP (Ainsworth et al., 1978) is the gold standard measure of attachment, because of both its wide use and its previous validation across cultures.

Attachment is the central developmental challenge of the first 20 months of life (Sroufe, Egeland, Carlson, & Collins, 2005). Attachment to mother, father, and other primary caregivers remains important throughout middle childhood as the background to psychosocial development. At this time, relations with peers and teachers are the primary area of psychosocial development. In early childhood, there is the challenge (related to attachment) of developing a positive sense of self, of gender membership, and of belonging in one's wider family and social group (e.g., relations with grandparents, cousins, aunts, uncles, neighbors). With the transition to school comes the requirement to coordinate goals and plans with other children and new adults (i.e., teachers). Will earliest (and ongoing) attachments to primary caregivers impact these new relationships vital to child development? There is a wealth of evidence in support of past attachments remaining an ongoing influence, yet there is also evidence in support of new relationships subverting, or compensating for, earlier ones. The compensation narrative (e.g., positive restorative experiences) is the more hopeful one to be researched and understood, so that such experiences can be promoted. Yet the alternative narrative about adversities (e.g., domestic violence or traumatic loss) that can subvert attachment and healthy psychological development must also be studied so that their pernicious impacts can be prevented.

According to Del Giudice (Article 2, this issue), children growing up in more or less stable and predictable circumstances experience ongoing adherence to early-learned patterns of interaction *because* the early lessons continue to be a reliable source for predicting how others are likely to behave and the extent to which children can rely on others for support. Article 2 provides insight into the meaning for children of social contexts that are threatening and highly volatile. In such contexts, strategies and automatic (hidden) assumptions about the world must remain in flux, able to change quickly, in response to rapidly changing (very likely threatening) circumstances. The unstable context may be one that becomes significantly more or less safe, and knowing that the safety may change permits an understanding by researchers of what is called lawful or meaningful discontinuity of attachment. A move from security to insecurity should be anticipated when the context becomes suddenly threatening, while a move from insecurity to security should be anticipated when threats recede and support pervades. To the extent that attachment security is grounded in instinctual component behavior systems present in newborn humans (and other animals), seen in reaching and holding on behaviors, then attachment security is inherently self-righting. This is because the experience of ruptures becoming reliably repaired leads to hope, trust, and joy. And, accordingly, we should more often see moves toward, rather than away from, attachment security. Carefully planned longitudinal research can help further our understanding of these change processes, which so far have been more often speculated upon than directly observed.

But what measures of attachment should be relied on in research that includes children who are no longer infants or toddlers? Moss and Lecompte (Article 5, this issue) have relied heavily on the modified SSP (essentially applying the Ainsworth et al., 1978, procedure to children through 5 or 6 years of age) and assembled a large body of evidence showing that continuing to observe children's behavioral responses to separation and reunion is meaningful with respect to identifying those children who rely on disorganized (controlling–caregiving or punitive) strategies. And it is now well established that a child who is disorganized with a caregiver is highly likely to be emotionally dysregulated with peers and teachers (Brumariu, Article 3, this issue). With respect to the typical insecure patterns of attachment (avoidant versus resistant) as opposed to secure patterns, the modified SSP is much less useful. So, overall, it must be concluded that, in choosing a measure of attachment suitable to middle childhood, more may be gained by looking forward to adolescence and adulthood and embracing an interview methodology, as Zimmermann and Iwanski (Article 4, this issue) report doing. Also age appropriate are questionnaire self-report techniques. Both interviews and questionnaires depend on the age-appropriate task of asking young people what they think and feel.

Looking Ahead

Emerging issues in the field concern the "new" theory of differential susceptibility positing that not all children are similarly affected by their caregiving environments; rather, some children are greatly sensitive to or impacted by the caregiving context and other children are impacted hardly at all. The search for valid measures of this biologically based characteristic (distinct from but related to temperament), and no doubt variable in its expression, will be the subject of ongoing research for some years to come. This line of inquiry, which must include longitudinal research designs that span middle childhood, is certain to modify and illuminate our understanding of risk and resilience, as it will show if the child most at risk is also the child most likely to show resilience. For those children biologically primed to be very sensitive to the caregiving context, attachments should change readily as the context changes; for other children not very sensitive to the caregiving context, attachments may not change much at all over time.

A further important developmental research issue (addressed in the commentary by Bin-Bin Chen in this issue) is whether findings observed in a study of one cultural group (defined by socioeconomic, linguistic, or ethnic status) also apply to other groups. After more than 50 years of research, it can be fairly argued that secure attachments are universal. That is, wherever attachment has been studied across the globe, in places where there is no recent history of war or natural disaster and a good-enough environment can be assumed, secure attachment is observed 55% or more of the time. This percentage of security remains the norm across childhood, into adolescence and adulthood, and mental ill health is strongly associated with insecurity across the life span. Where cultural variations impact attachment is in respect of insecurity (e.g., in northern Europe, avoidance is more common than resistance, while in Japan and Israel, resistance is more common that avoidance).

Finally, Del Giudice (Article 2, this issue) summarizes the effects of gender on attachment questionnaire (but not interview) data insofar as girls/women trend significantly toward anxiety and boys/men trend toward avoidance—differences not seen in infancy, so arguably they are not of biological origin. In early childhood in respect to doll-play story stem responses, attachment security is a leveler when it comes to these gender differences; that is, 5-year-old boys and girls with a history of a secure attachment to mother showed similar midlevel prosocial responses, but girls with an insecure history showed significantly heightened levels of "sweetness" and boys with an insecure history showed significant deficits (Steele et al., 2003). In other words, attachment security appears to overwrite the dictates of stereotypical culture-based or gender-based assumptions. This finding suggests that attachment security is very much about autonomy—that is, freedom to explore and freedom to relate, coping well with risk, and embracing opportunities with joy.

References

Ainsworth, M. D. S., Blehar, M. C., Waters, E., & Wall, S. (1978). *Patterns of attachment: A psychological study of the strange situation.* Hillsdale, NJ: Erlbaum.

Sroufe, L. A., Egeland, B., Carlson, E., & Collins, W. A. (2005). Placing early attachment experiences in developmental context. In K. E. Grossmann, K. Grossmann, & E. Waters (Eds.), *Attachment from infancy to adulthood: The major longitudinal studies* (pp. 48–70). New York, NY: Guilford Press.

Steele, H., & Steele, M. (2005). The construct of coherence as an indicator of attachment security in middle childhood: The Friends and Family Interview. In K. Kerns & R. Richardson (Eds.), *Attachment in middle childhood* (pp. 137–160). New York, NY: Guilford Press.

Steele, M., Steele, H., Woolgar, M., Yabsley, S., Johnson, D., Fonagy, P., & Croft, C. (2003). An attachment perspective on children's emotion narratives: Links across generations. In R. Emde, D. Wolf, & D. Oppenheim (Eds.), *Revealing the inner worlds of young children* (pp. 163–181). New York, NY: Oxford University Press.

HOWARD STEELE, PHD, is a professor of psychology at the New School for Social Research.

INDEX

AAI. *See* Adult Attachment Interview (AAI)
Abraham, M. M., 16, 37–39, 96
Actis Perinetti, B., 55
Adaptive plasticity, 19
Adult Attachment Interview (AAI), 25, 101
Ahnert, L., 4, 24, 83, 86
Ainsworth, M. D. S., 2, 5, 6, 49, 64, 79, 102, 103
Alexander, K.W., 54
Allen, J. P., 2–4, 24
Anderson, A. R., 87
Anderson, G. M., 8, 37, 40
Anderson, S. J., 54
Angeleri, R., 18–21, 23, 26
Apetroaia, A., 4, 8
Appleyard, K., 83
Arsenio,W. F., 48
Aspelmeier, J. E., 3, 7, 8, 37
Atkinson, L., 32, 66, 70, 71
Auchus, R. J., 18

Baiocco, R., 32
Bakermans-Kranenburg, M. J., 25, 27, 32, 34, 38, 41, 64–67, 70–72, 83
Bancroft, J., 21
Bar-Haim, Y., 68, 71
Bassett, H. H., 33
Bauminger, N., 38
Beckett, C., 48
Behavior problems: externalizing, 64–66; internalizing, 66–68
Belmaker, R. H., 72
Belsky, J., 19–21, 24, 33, 48, 53, 65, 66, 72
Benenson, J. F., 24
Benjamin, J., 72
Bennett, C., 24
Benoit, D., 34, 66, 70, 71
Berlin, L. J., 83
Bernier, A., 51
Bernstein, R. M., 19
Bernstein, V. J., 6
Berthiaume, C., 66, 67, 68

Beyond the Parent: The Role of Other Adults in Children's Lives, 79
Bidell, T. R., 51
Blehar, M. C., 2, 5, 6, 49, 64, 102, 103
Bliss, L., 86
Bogin, B., 17, 18
Bokhorst, C. L., 27
Booth-LaForce, C., 25, 55
Borelli, J. L., 8, 38, 40
Bornstein, M. H., 97
Bortfeld, H. V., 54
Bosmans, G., 1, 3, 4, 6– 8, 11, 14, 32, 39, 40, 42, 52–54, 57, 94, 96, 97, 100, 101
Bosquet, M., 71
Bost, K. K., 9
Bovenschen, I., 51
Bowlby, J., 2, 32, 48, 49, 50, 51, 57, 64, 72, 96
Braet, C., 3, 4, 6, 7, 11, 39, 42, 52, 53, 54
Brand, A. E., 41
Brekelmans, M., 80
Brenning, K. M., 6, 7, 11, 39, 42
Bretherton, I., 3, 6, 7, 48–50, 53
Brock, L., 86
Broth, M. R., 71
Brown, G. K., 5
Brumariu, L. E., 2, 3, 5–8, 11, 25, 26, 31, 32, 35, 37, 39, 40, 42, 45, 55, 64, 66–68, 70, 71, 95, 100, 103
Brumbach, B. H., 20
Brussoni, M. J., 27
Buhrmester, D., 81
Bullock, B. M., 71
Bureau, J.-F., 7, 8, 64, 68–72
Burge, D., 53
Burger, O., 18
Burgess, K., 55
Buyse, E., 81, 84, 85

Cadima, J., 83, 86
CAI. *See* Child Attachment Interview (CAI)
Calkins, S. D., 41
Callerame, C., 55

105

Rapoport, J. L., 18
Richaud de Minzi, M. C., 96, 97
Richters, J. E., 3
Ridenour, T. A., 7
Ridgeway, D., 6, 7
Rimm-Kaufman, S. E., 79, 85, 86
Riskman, J., 5, 33
Rizza, M. G., 86
Rogosh, F. A., 71
Roisman, G. I., 9, 25, 27, 32, 64–67, 70, 71
Ronai, Z., 72
Roorda, D. L., 85
Rose-Kransor, L., 55
Rothbaum, F., 94, 96, 97
Rouse, M. H., 71
Rubin, K., 55
Rudolph, K., 53
Rutherford, H. J. V., 38
Rutter, M., 48

Saarni, C., 34, 35, 41
Sabol, T. J., 78, 80, 82, 83, 85, 86
Sagi-Schwartz, A., 52, 53, 55, 68, 71, 94, 96
Salemink, E., 4
Sasvari-Szekely, M., 72
Sbarra, D. A., 8, 37, 40
Schad, M. M., 24
Scheuerer-Englisch, H., 56
Schlegelmilch, A., 16, 37, 38, 96
Schlomer, G. L., 20
Schneider, B. H., 32
Schuengel, C., 27
Schwarz, B., 39, 42
Scolton, K., 55
Scott, S., 5, 33
Secure Base Script Assessment test, 8
Seibert, A. C., 3, 5, 7, 8, 11, 25, 26, 32, 35, 37, 39, 40, 42, 55, 67, 79
Sharp, C., 25
Shaver, P. R., 51
Shaw, D. S., 71
Shelef, K., 5
Shelton, K., 37
Shields, A., 34
Shirtcliff, E. A., 20, 21
Shmueli-Goetz, Y., 8, 25, 27, 56
Shulman, S., 24
Simard, V., 66, 68, 69
Simpson, J. A., 24, 33

Sims, B. E., 6
Sinclair, M. F., 87
Sinha, P., 48
Skinner, A. T., 97
Slaughter, J., 55
Smolla, N., 66, 67, 68
Snavely, J., 38, 40
Socioemotional adaptation, 70–72
Socioemotional problems, and middle childhood attachment: disorganized/controlling subtypes and maladaptation, association of, 69–70; externalizing behavior problems, 64–66; internalizing behavior problems, 66–68; overview, 64
Soenens, B., 6, 7, 11, 39, 42
Solomon, J., 65, 70
Sommerstad, R., 27
Sonuga-Barke, E. J., 48
Sorbring, E., 97
Spagnola, M. E., 69
Spangler, G., 36, 39, 41, 49, 51
Spieker, S. J., 66
Spilt, J. L., 84, 85
Spinrad, T. L., 34, 48
Spitz, B., 53
Sroufe, L. A., 24, 33, 40, 51, 68, 70, 102
SSP. *See* Strange Situation Procedure (SSP)
St.-Laurent, D., 5, 6, 64, 69, 72
Starr, L., 36, 39
Stazi, M. A., 27
Steele, H., 8, 35, 36, 56, 99, 101, 104
Steele, M., 8, 35, 36, 56, 101, 104
Steele, R. D., 9
Sterner, K. N., 19
Stipek, D., 9
Strange Situation Procedure (SSP), 6, 52, 101
Strasser, K., 51
Stroud, C., 36, 39
Stuhlman, M. W., 78, 81, 82, 84, 85
Stutz, M., 39, 42
Suess, G., 51
Supplee, L., 70, 71, 83

Talge, N. M., 36, 41
Tarabulsy, G. M., 64, 69, 72
Target, M., 8, 55, 56
Taylor, A., 26
Taylor, J., 39, 41

NEW DIRECTIONS FOR CHILD AND ADOLESCENT DEVELOPMENT

ORDER FORM SUBSCRIPTION AND SINGLE ISSUES

DISCOUNTED BACK ISSUES:

Use this form to receive 20% off all back issues of *New Directions for Child and Adolescent Development*.
All single issues priced at **$23.20** (normally $29.00)

TITLE	ISSUE NO.	ISBN
_____	_____	_____
_____	_____	_____
_____	_____	_____

Call 1-800-835-6770 or see mailing instructions below. When calling, mention the promotional code JBNND to receive your discount. For a complete list of issues, please visit www.josseybass.com/go/ndcad

SUBSCRIPTIONS: (1 YEAR, 4 ISSUES)

☐ New Order ☐ Renewal

U.S.	☐ Individual: $89	☐ Institutional: $416
CANADA/MEXICO	☐ Individual: $89	☐ Institutional: $456
ALL OTHERS	☐ Individual: $113	☐ Institutional: $490

Call 1-800-835-6770 or see mailing and pricing instructions below.
Online subscriptions are available at www.onlinelibrary.wiley.com

ORDER TOTALS:

Issue / Subscription Amount: $ _____

Shipping Amount: $ _____
(for single issues only – subscription prices include shipping)

Total Amount: $ _____

SHIPPING CHARGES:

First Item $6.00
Each Add'l Item $2.00

(No sales tax for U.S. subscriptions. Canadian residents, add GST for subscription orders. Individual rate subscriptions must be paid by personal check or credit card. Individual rate subscriptions may not be resold as library copies.)

BILLING & SHIPPING INFORMATION:

☐ **PAYMENT ENCLOSED:** *(U.S. check or money order only. All payments must be in U.S. dollars.)*

☐ **CREDIT CARD:** ☐ VISA ☐ MC ☐ AMEX

Card number _____Exp. Date_____

Card Holder Name_____Card Issue # _____

Signature _____Day Phone_____

☐ **BILL ME:** *(U.S. institutional orders only. Purchase order required.)*

Purchase order #_____
Federal Tax ID 13559302 • GST 89102-8052

Name_____

Address_____

Phone_____ E-mail_____

Copy or detach page and send to: **John Wiley & Sons, One Montgomery Street, Suite 1000, San Francisco, CA 94104-4594**

Order Form can also be faxed to: **888-481-2665**

PROMO JBNND

CPSIA information can be obtained
at www.ICGtesting.com
Printed in the USA
LVHW040733200120
644151LV00012B/1574